MADE IN GOD'S IMAGE

MADE IN GOD'S IMAGE

Discovering and developing the person inside

DEL OLSEN

PYRANEE BOOKS

Zondervan Publishing House
Grand Rapids, Michigan

MADE IN GOD'S IMAGE

This is a Pyranee Book
Published by the Zondervan Publishing House
1415 Lake Drive, S.E., Grand Rapids, Michigan 49506

Library of Congress Cataloging in Publication Data

Olsen, Del.
Made in God's image.

1. Self-respect—Religious aspects—Christianity.
I. Title.
BV4647.S43047 1986 248.4 85-20947
ISBN 0-310-46381-5

Edited by Carol Uridil
Designed by Ann Cherryman

Printed in the United States of America

86 87 88 89 90 91 91 / 10 9 8 7 6 5 5 4 3 2 1

To Mary,
who loves me
To Karen Hoyt and Karen Shackleford,
who helped me
To the lay counselors at New Directions,
who support me

CONTENTS

PREFACE

This book is the result of a series of workshops on self-image which I conducted in churches in the San Francisco Bay area. This book is to serve as a guide to a process of self-understanding and change. Before a person can change the way he thinks and feels about himself, it is necessary for him to look at the issues that affect self-image development. A person must know where he is and how he got there before charting a new course. For that reason the "homework assignments" or self-exploration exercises are an important part of this book. Changes don't occur by simply reading and memorizing ideas. Acting upon the intellectual tools gained is the key to self-awareness and personal growth. The more effort a person puts into the process of self-exploration, self-discovery, and self-guidance, the more he will get out of this book.

Poor self-image is not the only personality problem that afflicts people, but it is a basic one. Poor self-image often accompanies profound and deep psychological pathology. Workshops and self-help books are no substitute for therapy. Individuals experiencing high levels of emotional pain will probably find little relief for their problems by reading this book.

Growth, not therapy, is what people can expect to gain from the process suggested in this book. If you can accept criticism, are aware of your feelings and able to express them, get along well with people, and have some close friends, then you can expect to benefit from self-exploration and self-guidance.

This book is more than just what I have done; it is an expression of who I am. My dual career as pastor and marriage-and-family counselor has led me to a profound appreciation for the traditional Christian disciplines for spiritual growth such as worship, Bible study, prayer, etc., and the techniques of modern psychology. My emphasis is practical. I am more concerned with pastoral theology than with historical or philosophical theology, and I am not particularly interested in the great number of psychological theories which abound.

My reasons for setting forth my ideas, then, is my pastoral concern for the enrichment and development of the spiritual and personal lives of God's people. Whatever contributes to this within the framework of the biblical view of man and the expressed purposes of God deserves consideration. I believe that the tools of modern psychology can be very effective in the hands of Christian practitioners.

The process outlined in the self-discovery and self-development sections of this book would be most effectively used in a study group. The opportunity for sharing and receiving feedback adds an important dimension. We expand our awareness by hearing ourselves speak about ourselves, and listening to the responses of others as we share helps us with our blind spots. Reading this book, doing the exercises, and sharing with a friend will maximize self-learning. The exercises which ask you to imagine will be most effective if you have another person guide you. Or if possible, read, or have someone else read the instructions for the exercises into a tape recorder. Then play back the recording, imagining what the exercises ask.

PART 1.

Self-Image and Self-Esteem

Self-Image and Self-Esteem

Looking at the lovely, sad, angry young woman sitting before me, it was hard to believe what I knew I was about to hear. You are never quite ready for stories like hers. Her life had been a model of Christian success. She was a beautiful, bright, well-educated product of an outstanding Christian home. Her life was filled with blessings and happiness, until that black Saturday afternoon.

Her husband shared her strong Christian commitments. He also came from a Christian home, was active in Christian college groups, and participated with his wife in a local congregation in the San Francisco Bay Area. His career had taken off like a skyrocket and his future in electronics was very bright. He pushed himself, worked hard, and didn't talk much about his feelings, but there was no indication that he was deeply troubled by anything.

As we talked that evening, and the many evenings to come, the recurring theme was, "What could have happened?" Precisely what happened will be a mystery forever. One Saturday afternoon when she came home from work and opened the garage door, she found her husband's body hanging from the rafters. There was no note and no discernible problem that could be identified as sufficiently severe to precipitate this tragedy. The problem was within him. Part of it was an unrealistic expectation that he could handle everything, and that expressing feelings other than anger was unmanly.

The point is that being a Christian has to affect more than just our thoughts, behavior, morals and values concerning the world; our Christian faith also needs to affect the ways we relate to ourselves. The purpose of this book is to draw attention to the strong teaching of Scripture which instructs us (those of us for whom the Bible is authoritative) on how to relate to ourselves and to offer practical guidance in how to understand our self-image needs and what can be done about them.

WHAT ARE SELF-IMAGE AND SELF-ESTEEM?

Self-image is the mental picture or set of beliefs we have about ourselves. Who we are, our true self, is one thing. Our self-image is something else. Our true self, with all of our ability, potential, skills, feelings, hopes and aspirations, is God's gift to us. This is our reality—who we really are. Our self-image is how we see ourselves. Our true self is God given. Our self-image is learned and is not always learned accurately. Unfortunately, however, our self-image is all we have to operate with.

If I am driving down the highway and see a tree growing in the middle of the road, I am going to stop, swerve, or do something to keep from hitting the tree. There may be no tree there, but all I have to go on are my perceptions. If the way I view myself is as distorted as the way I view that highway, I am in trouble. If my level of ability in math is average, but I have the idea in my head that I am a mathematical wizard, I am going to be pushing myself in an area where I lack aptitude, skill and interest—making myself miserable because my image or my belief about myself does not match my true self.

We have a good positive, or accurate self-image when the way we see ourselves reflects our true self. (There may be exceptions to this with highly neurotic or psychotic people who are not in touch with reality.) The relationship between the true self and the self-image is similar to the relationship of a bank balance in a checking account and on the check register. If the balance on the register and that in the bank are the same we will not overspend. But if an error is made on the check register, we may overdraw the account or fail to take advantage of economic opportunities because we believe we have less money than we really do. Overextending ourselves or inhibiting ourselves are consequences of inaccurate self-images.

Jane, a young woman I have seen as a client, believes her father died when she was nine because he didn't love her. Her belief is, "If my father had loved me, he would not have died." She has the idea in her head that nobody is ever going to like her or love her and that she cannot do anything right. She lives with anxiety, fear, and apprehension about every kind of social situation, including going to high school because she thinks that everyone is criticizing and judging her. The root of her problem is that she believes a lie about herself. She must change that belief to be able to use her personal resources.

When our self-image is in good shape we are able to adapt, learn, change, and grow. In short, we are able to develop our true self. When we have a negative self-image we are unable to grow or learn. We become like Jane, who believes that she is unlovable, so all the efforts her mother, sister, and friends put into trying to love her do not affect her. Because she believes she is unworthy and unlovable she cannot accept their love and affection.

Self-esteem, the way we feel about ourselves, complicates our self-image. If we make negative judgments about ourselves, or believe negative information about ourselves and come to negative conclusions about ourselves, we will feel badly about ourselves. If our self-image is that we are unworthy, ugly, no good, incompetent, and unlovable, then our self-esteem will be poor and we will not feel good about ourselves. We may also feel angry at ourselves for being that way, angry at God for making us that way, or helpless because we don't see any way out. We may feel sorry for ourselves and the horrible mess we are in. If these things are true, we are in trouble. We have a real problem as to how we are going to make it in this world if we are as bad off as we think we are.

One of the reasons why self-image problems are deep, and at times hard to identify and change, has to do with the way in which self-image is learned. There are four ways in which we as human beings usually gather and process information about life, or ways in which we learn. The first is sensory; by what we see, hear, smell, taste, and feel by touch. For example, when we see a room, we have learned something about that room. We have a memory of it in our heads. If someone were to ask us about it, we could answer because we have seen it. This is learning by general sensory perception—by means of our five senses.

Another way we learn is though abstract thinking. This is the ability to use symbols and to make sense out of them, which involves both language and mathematics. There are people who solve problems about buildings and machines without seeing them. They work off drawing boards, computers, equations and numbers, and they can tell you whether the bridge will stand or fall, whether the building is safe, or whether a machine will perform a particular function without ever seeing them. We are able to learn and solve problems by abstract thinking.

A third way we learn is through our feelings. This is

primarily interpersonal learning—the way we learn about people. Our feelings toward others, and the feelings they have expressed toward us, help us know where we stand with each other. Our feelings are an important way of learning about life and essential to understanding people.

The fourth way we learn is the most difficult to define. It is referred to as intuition—the ability to know the whole of something before having learned the parts. It is the ability to walk into a family or a group of people and sense what is going on. Some people have well-developed intuitions. They can pick up very subtle clues, put them together and come to very accurate conclusions.

Our ability for abstract thought develops slowly. It takes about seventeen years of life to develop to our full intellectual capacity. But we learn a great deal before we have this intellectual ability. Infants are born with all of their feelings functioning. Every human feeling can be seen in the lives of young children. You know when they are angry, scared, upset, or irritated. The emotional channel is the primary means of learning for young children.

We learn a lot about life before we are aware that we have learned anything. Infants learn whether or not human beings are safe by the way in which their mothers hold them and by the way they are treated within the family. If we are irritated with them and push them away, they get the idea that they are not loved, wanted, or valued. If they are neglected they develop negative ideas about themselves and whether or not life is to be trusted.

Erickson says that the basic task in the development of children between birth to two years is the development of trust or mistrust about life. Can you trust adults? Will they take care of you? Is the world friendly or frightening? Do you feel you are liable to be hurt, or your well-being is in danger? Do you have to be on guard, anxious, and tense?

Or do you believe that life is basically good and that the people around you cherish, value, protect, and take care of you? These important lessons are learned before any of us can articulate what it is we have learned.

Since many of the things about ourselves began before we remember learning them, they seem to be a natural part of us, but they are not. They are learned. They are learned by precognitive methods and channels other than the channels of the intellect. Childhood is important because children are like sponges. They absorb what you pour on them, and are very vulnerable to input from the external world. They do not have the experience or the cognitive capacity to say, "That's not true." Few of us can say that until we reach adolescence. Childhood is especially important because our initial self-image is formed during these years.

No adult can understand his self-image and self-esteem without sifting through his childhood experiences. We need to do a lot of remembering and some reliving of childhood experiences in order to understand their impact upon us. Many problems we experience as adults are the results of unhealthy patterns and perceptions we learned as children and have never unlearned or relearned.

WHY ARE SELF-IMAGE AND SELF-ESTEEM IMPORTANT?

Each person's self-image is a mixture of both plusses and minuses, but somewhere it balances out to fall either into the negative or the positive side. There are people of both extremes. A person with a good self-image is comfortable with himself. He is confident in his ability, able to make decisions, enthusiastic about life, generally optimistic, and not limited by the prospect of failure. A person with a negative self-image is generally fearful, has difficulty making decisions, doubts his abilities, is cautious rather than willing to live expansively and take risks. He always counts the cost and is generally pessimistic (he will think about what can go wrong rather than what might go right). Generally this person's life is rather restricted. He is so security conscious that at times he can be perceived as being dull. He is generally insecure.

Another reason it is important to look at self-image and self-esteem is that they are filters through which we see things and interpret our experiences. This selective seeing and interpretation maintains our self-image. For example, when people feel inadequate and left out, they will always see flaws in what they have done. They will negatively compare themselves to other people, believe that other people are doing things better, and conclude that they are no good. They may be very competent, excel in many areas, and be liked by people, but all this will never be good enough for them. They will interpret their experiences in ways which will justify their negative self-image. They sabotage themselves because they can't seem to accept success. They work like crazy until they get close to their objective or goals, and then they suddenly lose interest in life and do such things as show up late for work, fail to do their job, or pick a fight with the boss. This is a dynamic in marriage as well as in professions and careers. There are things we have that we feel we really don't deserve, and until we believe that we deserve them we are not going to be able to receive them with enthusiasm, joy, and appreciation.

Positive experiences alone are not enough to change self-image. This is what frustrates those in Jane's family mentioned earlier. They try to give Jane positive reinforcement and experiences, but those experiences will mean nothing until Jane accepts them as positive and lets that message get inside. Many people are driven to achieve more and more, yet it means less and less. They socialize more and still are lonely. We have to interpret the information, especially the positive experiences, in ways that get inside in order for us to be able to enrich our self-image. It is as though some people sit at a banquet table with food before them but refuse to eat. To them the dishes are empty while to the rest of us the dishes are full. We are able to eat, be filled, derive energy and nourishment, and go out to accomplish and achieve in life. Other people sit at the same table filled with the same abundance, yet walk away hungry, weak, and empty because they have not even seen the food, let alone eaten it.

What is most important is not what happens to us, but our internal response to what happens. That internal response is what goes into the mind and heart, and comes out as either a positive or a negative conclusion about ourselves. The difference between a defeated and a victorious person is often determined by the words of interpretation given an event. Both positive and negative self-image, then, are self-reinforcing. People who have a positive self-image are going to see the positive side of things and will feel good about themselves. People who have a negative self-image are going to see the negative side of things and end up feeling negatively about themselves.

A poor self-image and low self-esteem—an inadequate or inaccurate view of ourselves coupled with negative feelings about ourselves, are psychologically and emotionally crippling, and will result in our feeling unlovable, valueless, and incompetent. In contrast, an accurate self-image and good self-esteem will set a foundation on which we can grow and mature into the people God intended us to be.

PART 2.

Personal Growth and Faith

Personal Growth and Faith

This book also attempts to encourage us to put some effort into integrating psychology and personal growth with our Christian faith. I would like to say at the outset that for me God's Word is authoritative. Our goal here is not to do something that is in any way contrary to the Word of God. I believe that a good self-image is essential to spiritual growth and maturity. One of the aims of the gospel is that we grow and strengthen ourselves emotionally and psychologically as well as intellectually and spiritually. The gospel has an impact upon the whole person—no part of us is outside God's caring.

The presence of God in personal growth and development is found in the person and work of the Holy Spirit—the One called alongside to guide and support. There are many functions the Holy Spirit performs in the lives of people, but the predominate ministry is that of the Paraclete, the encourager of the brethren. The goal of the Spirit's work is to develop our full personhood after the model of Jesus Christ. Our task is to cooperate consciously and intelligently with the Holy Spirit to bring to full fruition all the possibilities given us by virtue of the first and second births.

The heart of the issue is responsibility. The humanist claims that man is solely and totally responsible for his growth and development. Some Christians say it is all

God—if He wants me to change He will do it. In Galatians 6 Paul makes two apparently contradictory statements. In verse 2 he states that we are to bear one another's burdens and in verse 5 he says that each of us shall bear our own burden. Applying this to personal growth and development, there are things God wants us to do for each other, but there are some things He expects us to do for ourselves. As a counselor I find myself telling some people, "You must do this for yourself, God will not do it for you" and to others, "Trust in the Lord, He is at work in this situation." God's Spirit is always at work, but wisdom and discernment are needed to see what God wants us to do for Him, others, and ourselves, The subject of self-image focuses on what God expects us to do for ourselves. I am not advocating "me-ism," but rather placing Christian responsibility on ourselves. Some books speak of our moral and ethical responsibilities to others, and others address our worship and service to God. This book emphasizes principles and processes that will develop a healthy relationship to ourselves. Some of the processes for self-discovery and change are from psychology, but the relationship principles are from Scripture.

We should have a high regard for ourselves. We are created in the divine image and that creation was affirmed as good. God did not create man and say, "Oh, I blew it. Back to the drawing board, mash the clay, and try it again." His creation was good, and the fall of man—man's disobedience to God—did not destroy man's worth. It destroyed many things, but it did not destroy our inherent and intrinsic worth as God's creatures. The doctrine of redemption is based upon God's valuing us. Sin—our disobedience and rebellion against God—can rob us of many things, but never our worth.

All human beings are valuable. Just as a gold coin can be dropped into a sewer and lose its effective use, it nevertheless remains a gold coin, intrinsically valuable. It is important in church circles to distinguish between people and their behavior. There is behavior that is contrary to God's will, which needs to be changed; but the person is always loved by God.

The gospel thrust that calls man to accountability and responsibility by pointing out our sin does not mean, and should never be interpreted that we as human beings are worthless. It does point out that we are in danger and vulnerable creatures. In the freedom that God has given us we have the capacity to destroy and inflict injury to ourselves, to other human beings, and to God's created order. It is as though we, as creatures, need a map to make it through life, or that we have been handed a machine we do not know how to work and we need the instructions. God has given us these in His Word as an expression of His love for us and His care for our well-being.

Many churches emphasize man's need rather than his potential. Man's capacity for evil is underscored rather than his capacity for good. Churches often exploit feelings of guilt, not to help us grow, but to control us. The motive is to keep us attending services, giving, and serving the goals of the organization, rather than helping us mature, grow up, and be able to stand on our own two feet as free men and women under the guidance of the living God.

Many times we confuse a positive self-image for conceit; that is, if people feel good about themselves that means they are going to run around bragging about themselves. Scripture admonishes us to think of ourselves with sober judgment in accordance with the measure of faith God has given us (Rom. 12:3). It does not honor God to discount the gifts and talents He has given us. To acknowledge value, even our own is not to be swell-headed or self-centered. On the contrary, bragging is a clue to a poor self-image. It is a compensatory behavior.

People who feel good about themselves do not have to convince either themselves or others as to how worthwhile they are. If we are valuable, we can accept our value without building up ourselves through tearing down other people, whether by judgment or criticism. We do not have to build up ourselves with flattery, self-deceit, or self-praise.

I think that Christian theology underlies any attempt to speak to the worth and lovability of man. To put it another way, one of the fundamental tenets of psychology is that you need to be able to tell a person he or she is worthwhile as a person. If, however, there is no God, and if we are just bits of boisterous scum on the surface of one small planet, the most that we can honestly say existentially would be, "I think you are O.K., but I don't know what Jim thinks, what Daryl thinks, or what Lou thinks, but I think you are O.K.; however, there is no assurance that you really are." Thomas Oden points out that there is not a therapist on the face of God's earth, atheist or Christian, who does not tell people that as human beings they are worthwhile. A therapist does not say, "I think you are worthwhile, but this is only my opinion." Rather he speaks as though he is a representative of reality. The Christian faith undergirds the whole therapeutic enterprise—without it there is no way that we can say that another person is worthwhile and of infinite value. Our true identity and sense of worth are found in realizing that we are children of God, created in His image.

Psychology and theology usually go hand in hand. When we strengthen ourselves psychologically and emotionally those insights invariably show up in our abilities to perceive spiritual truths. As we grow in both ways it is mutually reinforcing.

There are times when people cannot believe that there is any good in themselves until they experience in a very profound, mystical way the love of God in Christ. For others who have been Christians for years it is not until they go into counseling or another therapeutic experience that they understand God loves them and that they are valuable just as they are. It happens one way with some people and another way with others. It depends on where you are and what you need as to which of the two is more effective.

One of the clearest examples of the direct relationship between positive self-image and self-esteem is the Christian challenge of living by faith. Living by faith demands a willingness to take risks. The cautious and insecure person demands certainty and tends to reduce Christian living to formulas and rules, or legalism. Christian living is a journey in which we have no guarantees except that God loves us and is working out His purpose in our lives. To trust in the goodness of God and courageously live in a fallen and dangerous world requires confidence in ourselves as well as in God.

There are times when I encourage people to pray. There are other times when I tell people to stop praying because I am sure God is tired of listening to them whine about something that they already know how to take care of. Why should they waste their time and God's when they are really only scared to try. The real issue is that they want God to do something that is their responsibility, and until they accept this responsibility they will not grow.

Not only do a poor self-image and negative self-esteem distort our views of self, others and life, they also affect our perceptions of God in Christ. If we think we are unlovable and worthless, we will distort the messages of love and exaggerate the messages of judgment. A person who feels he deserves punishment will overidentify with evil and see Christ only as judge and executioner. Our human experiences affect the way we read and understand the gospel. I read about a city church that had a group of ghetto kids on a religious retreat and the leader was telling them about God as Father when one kid blurted out, "If God is like my old man, then I hate Him."

A negative self-image tends to provide a filter that selectively perceives and interprets things negatively. A person with a positive self-image is able to rejoice and see more of the goodness and grace of God than someone who has a negative self-image. He will be able to appropriate more of the gospel for his own benefit and the enrichment of others.

In summary, the doctrines of creation and redemption should promote a good self-image. We are valued and loved by God. If the gospel does not affect our self-image, it is not very deep within us. It has not penetrated or influenced us a great deal. We need to get our faith from our head to our heart where it will affect our behavior and our lifestyle, where it will become more than just a good idea that we think about. Then it will become a value by which we are able to live. Christian growth and maturity call for discipline and change. In order to change, to discipline and to monitor our own growth we need a positive self-image. A poor self-image deters growth. It discourages us from trying. To grow as Christians we need to learn new ways of doing things. We need to be willing and able to lay aside old defenses, to analyze ourselves, and take the risks that are called for to be new men and women in Christ.

PART 3.

Discovering the Person Inside

Discovering the Person Inside

All of us were children at one time, and most of us had parents who raised us. Thus, there is a part of us we can refer to as our internal child and also a part we can refer to as our internal parent—to a large extent we have internalized these parts from the way we experienced our parents and the world as children. These two elements are visitors from the past who still reside within us. The unique, up-to-date, in-touch-with-reality part of us we refer to as the adult.

For most of us, particularly if we have a somewhat negative self-image and self-esteem, the way we think and feel about ourselves is strongly influenced by those elusive visitors of the past—our child and our parent—who are not in contact with the here and now. This is why people who accomplish many things, who are attractive, loved and appreciated by many, can still feel ugly, unloved, and like failures. They are being dominated by voices of the past that speak so loudly they cannot hear all of the applause in the present.

All of us try to recreate in the present the emotional atmosphere of our past. This is what Missildine, in his classic book *Your Inner Child of the Past,* refers to as the "at home" feelings. That feeling, that emotional atmosphere from our childhood, may be one of fear, rejection, or insecurity, or it may be one of specialness, encouragement, or love. Whatever it was, positive or negative, we will seek to recreate it because it is only then that our inner child will feel "at home." However, this has been learned and it can be unlearned. That is the reason we now focus our attention on how the child develops and what the inner child needs. This will help us understand what we need to do to reparent or change our internal relationships. It will also help us be more sensitive and helpful in attending children around us, and the child we encounter in other adults.

CHILDHOOD

More has been written about childhood than any other period in life. In fact, there are so many theories and so much material available about children and raising children that the most we can do here is give a simple overview of childhood and why it is so important in developing self-image. We will look at the critical issues that impinge upon the development of self-image within ourselves, our children, our grandchildren, and people we influence.

There have been roughly eighty years of scientific study of human behavior, and during the first fifty of those years children were thought to develop because of mysterious forces at work inside them. If the children turned out well the parents were congratulated, and if they turned out lousy the parents were pitied. At that time it was thought that development was the result of genetic forces or blood or spirits, and the environment had relatively little to do with the way children turned out.

Then in the 1950s, because of Dr. Spock's theories, there was a 180-degree turn—the environment became the reason for everything. Children were viewed as being blank slates on which parents wrote the script of their lives. Before this time, parenting had been viewed as relatively unimportant, suddenly it became crucial. Parents were told that they were totally responsible for the way their children developed.

Today we realize that both heredity and environment are important. Some people are able to overcome miserable environments and turn out to be well-put-together human beings. Others live in excellent environments yet seem to have difficulties and problems that the environment cannot account for.

Good parenting is more an art than a science. That is, there is no set pattern for good parenting. The wisdom of Kenny Rogers' "Ballad of the Gambler" is often the way it is with parenting. You need to have the wisdom to know when to do what because there are times to be firm and there are times to be lenient. There are times to be gentle and there are times to be tough. You need to be able to perceive when those times are, and with every child they come at different periods in life. Although parenting is not everything, it is very important.

The critical issues which affect what children believe and feel about themselves are parenting functions. The following list is not exhaustive, but they are six extremely important issues. As stated earlier, self-image is learned. It is the result of the appraisals which children see mirrored in the people around them, mainly their parents. Therefore it is very important how children perceive their parents feel about them.

LOVE

Children need love. If they do not receive love, their self-image will suffer. The emotional warmth extended toward them, and the cherishing they experience in the arms and care of their parents, is essential. If our parents are delighted with us and love us then we know that we are lovable. If our parents are distant, cold, aloof and indifferent to us, we wonder whether or not we are lovable and worthwhile. If they are hostile toward us, sadistic, cruel, neglectful and abusive, we walk away feeling that we are worthless. The emotional climate in which we are raised is significant because we internalize it. If our parents enjoy us, if they delight in us and respond positively toward us, we think and feel good about ourselves. We believe that we are valued for being ourselves. If we do not value ourselves we cannot value others. We have difficulty making it through life if we feel unloved and worthless.

The root of much delinquent behavior lies in being unloved and uncared for. If we do not care for ourselves and do not care for others, then law and order, matters of justice, ethics, and morality mean little to us and provide little restraint for antisocial behavior. One of the most important things we can do for our children is to communicate that we love them for who they are.

There is much debate and talk about what love is. The definition of love that I like to work with is that we can say we really love someone when we are as concerned about meeting their needs as we are about having our own needs met. That works for marriage, parenting, and friendships. Caring is a matter of seeing that other people's needs are met. If we really love our children we are going to make sure their emotional needs are met.

ACCEPTANCE

The next critical issue in childhood is acceptance. A child needs to feel that his uniqueness and specialness are valued. Our judgments tell a child what he should be. Acceptance encourages him to be himself. The task of parents is not to imprint themselves upon their children or have them grow up as extensions of themselves. The task of parents is to help each child discover who he is and to develop himself in the best way possible.

Children need training in expressing themselves in socially acceptable ways. But the trainer need not be so rigid that the child does not feel good about himself if he breaks a rule or if he does not measure up. If we overemphasize the rules with controlling behavior, children grow up with no toleration of mistakes, and with perfectionistic expectations that if they don't measure up they are going to be punished. Such children cannot accept their humanness or allow others to know their weaknesses and pain. Their self-image is wrapped up in meeting the expectations of other people and not in valuing the uniqueness and the specialness of who they are. These unrealistic and high expectations keep them feeling badly about themselves. It is as though they are never quite good enough, or never measure up, and therefore can never be O.K. They always have to be working to be something else or something in addition to what they are. Every human being needs to find a balance between the importance of what others want him to be and what it is that he wants and expects from himself.

Another aspect of acceptance has to do with our feelings. The acceptance of our feelings is the most important validation of the self that we experience as human beings. If people do not accept and understand our feelings it is as though they are rejecting the most personal and significant part of our being. If our feelings are not accepted then we learn to repress and deny them, and we do not develop well emotionally as persons. Children seek internal consistency. If, by the way we treat them we cause them to feel like failures, they will probably fail. If we treat them and teach them to be winners, they will probably win. It becomes a self-fulfilling prophecy. If we feel good about ourselves we are more likely to have positive achievements and accomplishments. If we feel poorly about ourselves we will more likely avoid success and seek failure. We live to conform to and meet the demands of our self-image.

DISCIPLINE

Children feel secure as a result of both love and discipline. Discipline basically says, "I care enough to set limits and to follow through with them." It also tells the child that his environment is dependable. He learns what he can expect—that life is not capricious and that it makes sense. If he obeys the rules he will receive a certain reward. If he disobeys the rules there are certain consequences. A child learns what to expect from life and also to be responsible for his own behavior.

We get into a lot of trouble with the issue of self-image and discipline. The purpose of discipline is to teach, not to hurt. The focus of discipline should be on the behavior, not on the person. A person should never use labels that demean a child. Yes, some behavior may be foolish, inappropriate, and ineffective, but that does not mean that children are liars, cheats, creeps, stupid, and no good. Such statements describe lasting characteristics that children learn to believe about themselves and may have lasting consequences. Children lack the intellectual development and experience needed to evaluate such statements and reject them. They are not able to decide what is true and what is not true. Discipline and protection have to do with the way parents use power.

In our role as parents, we can be authoritarians which means "Do it because I said do it and don't ask any questions. That's just the way it is." Such use of power tends to breed dependency, overconformity, or rebelliousness on the part of the child. The problems of the overconforming child are often more severe than the problems of the rebellious child. It is usually the rebellious child who gets the attention. That is the child taken down to see the counselor or the minister or Uncle John or somebody to try to help set him or her straight. The overconforming child is more likely to have deeper and longer-term problems.

The other inappropriate role parents take is the role of permissiveness where the child possesses the power. Parents are more concerned with being buddies than with being parents. The child is left with the questions, "Is anybody here in charge?" and "Who besides me counts?" If the child gets what he wants and does what he wishes, he thinks the whole world is centered around him and becomes self-centered, indulgent, and unprepared to deal with the limitations that he is going to face throughout life. Discipline in the home helps a child live with frustration, disappointment, and anger in a setting where he is loved. A child who does not experience this and fails to learn to deal with these emotions has a rude awakening when he becomes an adult. It is hard to deal with frustration if you have not been taught how with love.

PROTECTION

Parents must also offer their child protection. Parents must be willing to speak up or act in order to keep their child's person or rights from being violated. This includes protection from bullies, public school teachers who may treat the child unfairly, and parents of other kids who may berate the child. Parents should be willing to offer protection for their child and to help work out the problem.

One of the horrible memories I have from childhood is of a summer evening in the housing project where we lived in Barstow when I was about thirteen or fourteen years old. Summer evenings were nice there. You could see the stars and breathe the air, but there wasn't much else to do. However, we had a couple pairs of boxing gloves and under the clothesline we had fixed up a boxing ring. We would each go in and go a round or two with one another, and we'd take turns being referee in order to keep the big ones from killing the little ones. On this particular night we were boxing, and one of the younger boys didn't want to box because he had a headache. Someone had hit him on the side of his head and it really hurt. After a while, his father,who had been drinking that evening, came down to watch the kids box. He started goading his son to get in there and box. The boy said, "I don't want to. My head hurts." So his dad started calling him names and when that didn't work he offered a quarter to anyone who would hit the boy. He offered no protection for the rights of his child.

As a child it didn't seem that important to me. But now that I have grown up the failure of that father to use his manhood, strength, and wisdom to guide and protect his son, seems like a terrible injustice. If the boy didn't know how to fight, his father should have taught him rather than bully him. The father became a threat instead of a protector.

If parents overprotect, children won't develop self-confidence. They won't learn to speak up for themselves or fight for themselves. It's a fine line; if children do not get enough protection they will feel intimidated and overwhelmed by life. Again, it is an art with each child to give enough protection that he or she knows he is important and yet not so much protection that he never has to deal with anything and therefore goes through life feeling like someone is always going to come along, bail him out or rescue him. That way he never has to deal with or face the difficult circumstances of life.

Children feel insecure if parents do not defend the family's borders. They need to be safe from physical and psychological assault. If parents help defend them then they will learn how to defend themselves. They will also learn that they are worthwhile and that their well-being is important. Not only do parents need to be concerned about protecting children from assault and problems outside the family, but within the family there is the need for evenhanded administration of justice in guiding the affairs of the family. Parents should avoid the temptations to favor the boys or to favor the girls, to favor the youngest or to favor the oldest, to favor the strongest or to favor the weakest, to favor the smartest or to favor the dumbest. Each child needs to know that he or she is in good standing in our affection and that we do not play favorites, allowing some to get away with things not allowed by others. The way in which children are treated within the family has a powerful effect on the way they feel about themselves.

One of the reasons why protection is so important—and this may be the most important thing that I have to say about children, and it applies to a number of these areas, not just the issue of protection—is that we cannot treat the hurts, slights, and insults a child experiences in the same way we do with an adult. An adult can evaluate a slight, an insult, or a hurt by taking into account the source, what the motives might be, and looking back over his own history of things to decide, "Other people do not treat me that way, why should I take it from you?" As adults we can evaluate the feedback we get and decide how much we are going to take in. Children do not have that kind of intellectual discernment nor that sort of experience. So what children do—and this is the part of it that lies at the root of a lot of adult pathology because children have no experience by which to validate or disclaim information—

is to project the experience into the future and believe that it is always going to be that way. They believe that they are always going to feel hurt and that people will always take advantage of them. Therefore they develop the defenses of being guarded, suspicious, and fearful in the way they relate to people.

INDEPENDENCE

Parents need to encourage their children's independence by affirming their achievements and abilities to do for themselves, to master their environment, and to control themselves in order to gain personal strength and competency. The best behavior-shaping tool parents have is rewarding good behavior and not rewarding bad. People tend to repeat behavior that is rewarded. Parents who reward good behavior and encourage intellectual and emotional independence raise children more likely to become independent adults.

Children need to experience the trust of their parents. This is crucial to the development of self-image. Parents who trust their children and affirm their independence by giving them tasks that stretch their competencies, allowing them to try and perhaps to fail, show respect for them and build their self-confidence.

Overly protective parenting is the clearest and most obvious hindrance to a child's developing independence. Insecure parents often overstructure the child's life with rules and regulations. Other parents have such strong fears of harm coming to their children that they cannot allow the reasonable risks that are necessary to let a child test his limits. Less obvious, but far more damaging, are parents who seek to live through their children. They see their children as an extension of themselves and thus cannot allow them to be independent in thought, feeling, or action.

Finding the balance between adequately structuring a child's world and overcontrolling it is part of the fine art of parenting. The self-image consequences for the child are significant. The message from the overprotective parent is, "You can't handle it; the world is too much for you." The message from the enmeshed parent is, "It's my life that counts, not yours." In neither case is the child able to achieve psychological independence.

GENUINE ENCOUNTER

The last thing that I want to say about issues in childhood concerns basic, genuine encounter with adults. We need to spend time with our children, letting them know what we think and what we feel. It is important for them to see our humanness and know our failures. We can reduce the competency gap between children and adults by not trying to appear perfect, righteous, or all-powerful. We need to let them know that we have weaknesses and that in some ways they are better than we. This goes a long way toward building self-confidence in our children.

I play tennis every Wednesday with a friend, and one of the most disgusting experiences that I have had was the day we saw and heard a father and son playing tennis in the next court. The father was a loudmouthed braggart. He teased his son and laughed at him when he made mistakes. And even worse, the father cheated. He would argue with his son about shots of his that were obviously out. He also argued over the score. In fact, the father kept the score written down. There were times when I wanted to say, "Why don't you let your son keep the score?" All this happened because it was so important for the father to win. His own ego needs were so great that he could not appreciate and value his son across the net who loved him so much that he was willing to put up with all this just to be with him. This incident made me both angry and sad. It was sad because this father failed to realize what a loyal son he had.

In contrast, one of the best things that I had heard in a long time was of a man who married a woman with three children, the oldest being a boy who was somewhat of a problem. Shortly after the marriage this boy cut school and the wife said to her new husband, "I've had it. You deal with him." I asked this father what he did and he said, "Well, I took him outside and the first thing I did was tell him about the time I cut school." This father didn't try to be perfect. He tried to reduce the competency gap so the son would know that he was not the only person in the world who had ever cut school, yet the father also told him that it was abut the dumbest thing he had ever done. Before he got down to teaching and disciplining, he was willing to identify with the boy.

Meeting a child's emotional needs as a parent, and reflecting a clear and positive self-image requires a great deal of strength and maturity. Parents with poor self-images are distorted mirrors for their children. Over and over again I tell parents who bring their children in for me to talk to, that if they work on themselves, the child will be fine. Take care of yourselves and be good models, and in most cases the children will follow. It is terribly important for parents to assume this kind of responsibility.

These six elements—love, acceptance, discipline, protection, independence, and genuine encounter—are not only important to understand and use in our relationships with our children, grandchildren, Sunday school students and other children, but they are absolutely crucial to how we relate to ourselves. Each of us was at one time a child, and to a large extent that child we were is still an active part of our personality. Understanding our internal child is essential to understanding and eventually changing a negative self-image and self-esteem.

EXERCISE FOR UNDERSTANDING THE CHILD INSIDE

In this exercise I want you to reflect upon your childhood experiences prior to age twelve. First, write down some of your earliest memories, such as preschool, first grade, etc. Shift your brain into neutral and let memories surface as you think about your childhood. What are the things that come up,what are the memories? Specifically think about the following:

1. What was the emotional climate of your childhood?
2. What feelings stand out for you? What were the major feelings that you experienced on a consistent basis as a child? Were they feelings of fear or anger or pleasure?
3. How were you praised and punished by your parents? When your father praised and punished you, how did he do it? What did he say? What were you praised and punished for? Do the same thing for your mother.
4. Write a paragraph describing each of your parents. And if there was another significant adult, such as a grandmother or grandfather who was instrumental in your rearing, also write a description of them. What kind of people were they and how did you relate to them?

You will probably write several pages as you comb your memories and go through your recollections of childhood. Are there any issues from your childhood revealed from this assignment that still trouble you and that you would like to change?

ADOLESCENCE

Adolescence,that period between the ages of twelve and twenty is a time when the teenager is doing graduate work on childhood. He is trying to take his experiences as a child and make them work in an adult world. The six issues of childhood—love, acceptance, discipline, protection, independence, and genuine encounter—are still very important. But added to these are emerging sexuality, career indecision, the conflict between dependence and independence, tremendous biological and emotional changes, and a new sense of power.

The teenage years or period of adolescence is that period of transition from childhood to adulthood. The one word to describe adolescence is "change." The reason why adolescence is such a turbulent and threatening time is because there are so many changes at so many different levels. In childhood everything is pretty much predictable. But by age thirteen or fourteen the world is upside down because everything is changing; there are intellectual, emotional, spiritual and social changes.

Let's look at some of the changes which take place during adolescence and how these affect how teenagers feel about themselves and the development of their self-image.

POWER

Adolescence has been referred to as the second age of negativism. The first one is the "terrible two's" when children find out that there is at least one thing that parents cannot make them do. When they get to be teenagers they find out that there are many things that parents cannot make them do. Between age two and the teenage years children are more conforming, more compliant, more positive in exploring and learning, and not very negative. But when they get to be teenagers, they suddenly become uncooperative. They want things their way rather than the parents' way or the way it has always been done in the family. Adolescents are coming into a sense of new-found power. At two what they begin to find out, in their emerging individuality, is that their parents, Godlike though they are, cannot control them totally. When they get to be teenagers they find out that there are more things parents can't control. Parents can't control their thoughts or feelings, and to a large degree parents cannot even control their actions because they are able to get out of sight. This new found power is tested and tried out.

This testing is essential for a teenager to grow up. It also reveals the quality of interpersonal life in the family. If ties of affection and respect for parents are strong, the testing will be moderate. Teens and parents will find that there is a balance between the needs of the teenager for new experiences and the needs of the family for loyalty, togetherness, and happiness. If family relationships are good, teenagers will not demand too much and neither will parents. Mutual respect and affection facilitate this balance.

INTELLIGENCE

A key area of change in teenagers is intellectual. Adolescents have an emerging capacity for abstract thinking. By age sixteen or seventeen this capacity is fully developed. Their minds can quickly grasp and understand facts. They do not have a lot of wisdom or experiences with which to process information, but they are quick to acquire information. Along with this—and this is the part that affects self-image and personality so much—comes the ability to see oneself objectively and separate from others. Teenagers can see themselves as separate from what they do and become aware of the difference between what goes on in the world outside and what goes on inside themselves. The world of childhood is immediate. When something happens a child's response is reflexive. Children don't stop to think. If they hurt, they cry. Teenagers may get hurt and not cry because they have learned how to control their responses. They know they can put on a mask and not let people know what is going on deep inside them. They are able to observe and analyze the world, and can observe and analyze what is going on inside themselves and differentiate between the two.

With this capacity for self-examination (at times a preoccupation with one's own feelings and thoughts) is an emerging self-consciousness. Teenagers are extremely self-conscious. They think others are looking at them with the same critical view that they use when looking at themselves. This is one reason why peer pressure is so intense. Adolescents are very concerned about the way other people think of them. The opinions of other people become very important. As we begin to grow up we realize that other people aren't spending all their time scrutinizing us, so we relieve ourselves of that burden, go off to be ourselves, and don't worry so much about what other people think of us. But while our identity is being formed the opinions of other people are important to us.

Children who are overly conforming tend to suppress themselves, but as their identity begins to form as teenagers they have a choice: are they going to suppress and deny themselves in order to be accepted by other people, or are they going to be themselves and take chances as to whether or not other people are going to accept them? Many times the conforming child ends up having more personality problems than the rebel because the conforming child often sells his or her own individuality, sacrificing it for approval. The rebellious child tries to establish his identity and often gets help doing this because of all the noise he makes. The thinking of a conforming child is that if other people say he is O.K., then he is O.K., rather than thinking, "Hey, I think this is right so this is what I am going to do. And if they don't like the way I do it, then I am sorry." For the teenager, as for all of us, the need is to find the balance between personal integrity and the needs and desires of others.

Another thing that happens during this period is that teenagers do cognitive framing of their self-image that comes out of their childhood. They think about the sort of person they are and many times, if their self-image is positive, they will affirm it intellectually and say, "Hey, I believe I am a really neat person." They will put words to it rather than just pictures or feelings, developing a more rational, cognitive context. But the negative ideas and feelings can also be affirmed. Cognitive framing makes things seem more real, important, and strong. Self-image gets worse or better as a result of the process. We can dig the hole deeper than it was in childhood or sometimes we can reflect on ourselves and work our way out of negative feelings from childhood.

Teenagers often develop a style of living to adapt to a negative self-image. They feel worthless, and rather than working on the worthlessness they engage in compensatory behavior such as becoming class clowns, drug users, braggers, and sexually promiscuous. An example of this was a client I saw several years ago who had a traumatic, embarrassing, and humiliating experience during childhood. At that time he decided to never let people put him on the spot again. To protect himself he started lying to his mother. This practice became generalized during adolescence when he began developing a double life—telling people what they wanted to hear and then doing as he pleased, covering his tracks with deception. The problems this created were much worse than facing any of his reality directly. Rather than dealing with his feelings of powerlessness and helplessness he chose to stay with the strategy of protecting himself that he developed during his teenage years. That strategy has been an enormous problem in his adult life. Until he chooses to update his self-image he will be compelled to deceive and manipulate in order to survive.

PHYSICAL CHANGE

The next big area of change is physical. During adolescence there is rapid physical growth—spurting up, spurting out, emerging sexuality, clumsiness, a keen awareness of the body, acne and blemishes, being too tall, too short, too fat, too slim. Each of these brings about different problems. I doubt there is any teenager who fully accepts himself or herself. There is always something wrong and teens are very sensitive to ridicule and rejection. Both have a powerful impact on how teens perceive themselves. If people ridicule them or put them down during this vulnerable time when they are half man and half boy, half woman and half girl, it can have a long-lasting negative impact.

Acceptance of the body and the self are closely related. The body is an extension of the person and our means of contact with the real world. Much of our communication with other people is nonverbal. If the body conveys messages of non-O.K.ness then the response from teenage peers (insecure themselves) can be quite negative. It is difficult to be self-accepting and understanding when the peer group isn't. That is why the security, understanding, and affirmation of family is critical to the adolescent's sense of well-being.

SEXUAL DEVELOPMENT

Sex is another big issue. Teenagers experience powerful feelings and impulses and wonder how to cope with their sexual drives. Society and parents say no, and their bodies say yes. What are they going to do? It is a period in life when they are least able to cope with these impulses, yet they don't have any choice. Sexuality has to be coped with during the teenage years before their identity is formed, before their value structure established, before they really know who they are, and while they are susceptible to peer pressure, ridicule, and rejection. Sex has to be dealt with because the feelings are as intense as they will be at any period in their lives, yet teens are not very well equipped to deal with such feelings. It is important how sexual feelings are handled because the way teens view their maleness or femaleness is usually determined at this very vulnerable and crucial time in their lives.

The physiology of sex complicates things. Along with the sexual urges and feelings and excitement are the development of breasts, facial hair, menstruation, genital maturation, etc. At this point, nothing is ever quite right—too much, too little, too soon, too late. Between the inner and outer worlds of sexuality it may seem to teenagers that sex is everything. One task of growing up is to get sex into proper perspective and to avoid using sex as a channel for meeting emotional needs such as affection, approval, recognition, status, etc. Sex, in teenage culture, provides an attractive, exciting, and easy way to immediately and temporarily meet these needs.

Parents ask what they can do to help their teenagers through this period. One thing is to try to understand teenagers' feelings and let them know that you went through it too. Let them know that people do manage to survive and that adolescence is not a life sentence. It is not a permanent condition. The second thing is to help teenagers develop a good self-image, affirming them. That is the best antidote to peer pressure and will help teens maintain their own moral standards.

There is another reason why the guidance, sharing, and affirmation of parents is crucial to teenagers. By talking openly about sex with our children, we dispel much of the allure of the forbidden and provide valid information to counter the misinformation they absorb from the culture and the media. Parents who say "Don't grow up, don't be sexual, ignore it and it will go away," induce severe distortions in the psychosexual development that needs to take place during adolescence. Parental modeling is never more important than it is in the sexual development of children. We parents teach them what maleness and femaleness are all about.

DEPENDENCE-INDEPENDENCE

Another issue with teenagers is dependency. As children they were very dependent, as teenagers they are beginning to make the transition from dependence to independence. However, there is no clear-cut dividing line. It is not as if they are still children from thirteen to fifteen and then from sixteen on they are adults. It does not work that way. It is more a matter of percentages. One day they will act like adults and you think you can trust them with anything. The next day they will do the most impulsive, thoughtless things imaginable and you wonder where in the world their brains are. That back and forth behavior is part of being an adolescent.

Teenagers are moving toward psychological independence and autonomy, but they are not there yet. The task of parents is to encourage them the days when they are adults and accept the days they have to deal with children. Teens are not going to be consistent. Parents must accept this inconsistency.

One of the major reasons that parents of teenagers come in for counseling revolves around the issue of freedom. The teenager feels the parents are treating him like a nine-year-old—sometimes they are. The parents have not learned how to relax the rules and let the teen have more opportunities to learn from his own experiences. When he falls down, help him a little bit, but let his experiences be a guide for how much freedom he has. Parents should encourage teens toward independence by helping them learn to develop their own personal strength and competency.

Part of the phenomena of teenage rebellion is that teens want to be independent, but are afraid to be. They hold on under the table and strike out at parents for not letting go, not letting them have their own way, when to be independent all they have to do is let go from under the table and pull away. Whenever someone stands and bangs and fights for their rights in this position they are not asking to be independent. What they want to do is make a big scene to appear independent, yet avoid paying the price of going ahead and running the risk of falling down.

Some people say that rebellion is a necessary phase of adolescence. In contrast, I think that independence is a necessary phase of adolescence that is essential for teenagers. Many teenagers learn how to be independent and autonomous without rebelling. If parents do a good job in guiding their teenagers, rebellion should be minimal.

RELIGIOUS EXPERIENCE

Many teens come to Christ and make decisions with reference to their faith. I think this is definitely related to identity formation. It is a part of seeing ourselves as being responsible to God for our own beliefs, our own commitments, our own thrust in life apart from our parents. As teenagers begin to think about themselves and think about life, their spiritual concerns become very important. This is one area where teenagers are in control. No one else can control their thoughts, their religious convictions, their beliefs. Their parents may not like them going to church, but parents cannot keep them from believing if they want to. Unfortunately many times this gets tied into a rebellious cycle, such as if the family is Jewish the teenager is going to become Catholic just to upset the family tradition. Or if the family is a strong church-going family the teenager may decide to be an atheist. He will not believe like his parents want him to believe because that is one thing that parents cannot demand. Establishing religious beliefs may bring about rebellion or it can lead teens to sorting out who they are in this universe.

There are good reasons why people come to Christ and to his church during the years of childhood and adolescence. During these periods their intuition is very strong. In some ways we are spiritually more vulnerable and more approachable by God's Spirit then when we become more cerebral, more cognitive, more logical and analytical.

PEER PRESSURE

During the teenage years more social and personal needs are met outside of the family. Teenagers visit other homes and see how other people do things. It is a part of becoming aware of life and how other families function. Teens begin to develop their own ideas of how they want their family life to be and how they are going to treat people. Many times this exposure helps teens correct some of the negative things that go on inside their own families.

If the peer group is too important to the adolescent it may indicate a lack of nurturing at home. I think that basically teenagers want to cooperate with their parents. If they do not, there are usually good reasons, and many times it is not the teenager's fault. Often a lack of nurturing, of good parenting at home, drives teenagers to their peer groups to get their needs met. Where their needs are met is where their loyalties will lie. If their needs are met at home then they will be loyal to their families.

I recently talked to a man who gave up on his family a

number of years ago. He wasn't going to get a divorce, but it didn't seem worth the effort to try to work things out. He said it was amazing how little he remembered of over twenty years of marriage. But he could remember everything about work. He knew every move he made, every job he had, significant tasks, people who helped him, and people who hurt him. He had invested everything into his work because that is where his needs were met. He was financially responsible to his family but that was about all.

VOCATION

The last issue with teenagers that we will look at is the issue of vocation. That is the question "What can I do with my life? I have to decide what I want to be when I grow up and what course of action I am going to take." Teenagers need guidance at this point. They do not need demands from their parents, nor do they need to have decisions made for them. They need guidance in developing what it is they wish to do with their lives vocationally. It is important to a teenager's identity to have a sense of direction. I know this from raising my own sons.

Our oldest son was our slow bloomer. He had the most difficulty deciding what he wanted to be. Once he made that decision his college career took off. Our middle and youngest sons have always known what they wanted to do. Our middle son has always wanted to do something with his hands, to be a builder, and he has done it with little self-doubting. He wanted to work several years before going to college, but he is now enrolled in college. He learned the hard way that working without a degree is a dead-end street. He decided he wanted more out of life than that, but he had to learn it for himself. Our youngest son is a musician and the sense of knowing where he fits in life, what it is he can do and enjoys doing helps keep him focused. His career path has been the most direct of the three.

The whole process of vocational choosing is very complicated. First, there are so many options and choices. In the past, a young person only had two or three options. For a woman the options were to get married, be a missionary, a nurse, or a school teacher. A man didn't have much more to choose from. He either did what his father told him to do or he went to the next county and tried something else. Now there are so many options that the training period for developing skills in a good vocation takes many years.

It is important for parents to focus upon children's skills rather than upon roles. Parents need to allow children to live their own lives. Children aren't extensions of their parents. One of the most valuable things God ever taught me was when my oldest son was in his early teens and the other two were eight and ten. One day when I was frustrated and upset about what was going to happen to these boys, it occurred to me that these are not my children, these are God's children. They are not mine to own so my ego is not wrapped up in their performance. They are responsible to God. I am only responsible to God for being the best parent I can be for a particular period of time to give them training. I have already had my chance. Now I try to model consistently what I think is important for a Christian man to be, but I cannot assume responsibility for them or try to shape them into being what I want them to be. Too many parents try to live out their frustrated needs through their children.

Children should be encouraged in their dreaming process. Talk to them about their dreams and what they see themselves doing years from now. Take them seriously. Their ideas aren't necessarily God's last word to them,but I believe that all of us intuitively know more than we can explain about ourselves. Dreams and intuitions are ways knowledge speaks to our conscious minds. If we listen to that dialogue and take those pictures seriously they can be other sources of guidance for our lives.

CONCLUSION

The task of adolescence is to find out who we are, what we can do apart from our parents, and to whom and how we will give ourselves in affection, trust, and love. Adolescence is a time of insecurity. Few teenagers have a good self-image. Part of this is because they are moving from being the center of the universe as children to the place where parents expect them to pick up their rooms, make good grades, assume responsibility for themselves, and guide their own growth and development through making choices. Suddenly life becomes serious for teenagers. Parents say, "Find out who you are." That's fine, but when they look at themselves and see many selves, they wonder which self they are. Adults need to understand that and say "Hey, that's all right, there are lots of parts to each of us." The task is to get to know these parts and bring them into a harmonized unit so that we feel whole, not fragmented.

EXERCISE FOR UNDERSTANDING THE ADOLESCENT INSIDE

Spend some time looking at your period of adolescence, which includes the years from age thirteen to nineteen. Write a paragraph with about ten facts on each of the following six subjects.

1. Your relationship with your parents as a teenager
2. Your relationship with siblings if you had any
3. Your relationship with friends if you had any
4. Dating
5. School
6. Work

Then write descriptive comments about what adolescent life was like for you. It does not have to relate to any one of these subjects, but what was adolescence like for you? Share your feelings about it, if they were not touched in these other areas.

In doing this exercise have you discovered problems with your adolescence that still plague you? What are they? Would you like to change them? How would you like to change or resolve them?

ADULTHOOD

The task of adulthood is to harmonize and develop the parts of us that emerge from adolescence. Our identity is the result of how we organize these parts and how well they work together. One way of understanding personality is to look at each of us as being a group of three people in which our nuclear family, our family of origin, largely becomes internalized. There is a parent part of us, an adult part of us, and a child part of us.

THE INTERNAL PARENT

The parent part of us is basically a tape recording of all the rules and control messages we have received, including things that culture has taught us, such as boys don't do this and girls do that, or girls don't do this and boys do that. It is full of shoulds and oughts. The purpose of the parent is to provide guidance, protection, and control over the basic impulsive nature of the child. This is essential. Our parents, school, church, nation, the mores of the broader culture plus the idiosyncrasies of our own particular family are written into the internalized parent part of us enabling us to fit into society.

There are primarily two ways the internal parent

exercises control over us. One is by criticizing and the other is by nurturing. We all have some of each, but if we were raised in a critical environment where our parents demanded a great deal, held high expectations, and were critical of us, we probably internalized that critical element and tend to be harder on ourselves. We are more apt to treat ourselves in the same critical, demanding way our parents treated us. We talk to ourselves in critical ways. If our parents were warm, nurturing, and understanding, we probably internalized that and deal with the child part of ourselves in nurturing and understanding ways. We reinforce our positive behavior as well as criticize our negative behavior. The parent part of us is a tape recording by which we talk to ourselves and tell ourselves what is important in the dos and don'ts, what we should and shouldn't do.

THE INTERNAL CHILD

The internal child is also a tape recording, but it is an emotional tape. This child part of us is the repository of our emotions and is basically the child we have always been. As mentioned earlier, the adult part of us is practically nil when we are born. We cannot think, we cannot figure things out very well. However, the feeling part of us is active from the moment of birth and probably before. Like the core of an apple, a lot develops around it as the apple gets bigger, but that core inside, the center, remains essentially the same.

There are two types of children within each of us. There is the natural child who is spontaneous, adventuresome, fun-loving, creative, who enjoys the discovery of new things, and is uninhibited. The child part can also be cruel, demanding, selfish, and out of control. The purpose of the parent is to provide control without stifling the child's emotional energy and creativity. The natural child needs to be guided and disciplined, but not overcontrolled. The adaptive child is the child raised in a critical, demanding, rigidly structured or threatening atmosphere, who lives his or her life trying to please the expectations of the parents. All children need to adapt, but when children try too hard to please others they have difficulty finding out who they are. A woman recently said to me, "I was a good little girl and I hated it. I resented being so controlled because while I was living out other people's expectations I never found out who I was." She was an adaptive child who lived to meet the expectations of other people—this is a problem in her life now.

THE ADULT

The adult is the most distinctive and individual aspect of the self. Both child and parent parts of us are shaped by our childhood environment, voices from the past. But the adult part is built upon our own experiences, skills, and desires. In the mature personality the internal parent and the internal child are important, but neither of them are equipped to be in charge. If the child is in control we function impulsively, running on feelings without guidance. When the parent is in control we live as robots, seeking to please voices out of our past. Only the adult part of us has the resources for knowing our true self. The adult part thinks and chooses. It gathers and analyzes data, computes consequences, and makes decisions. The adult is in touch with reality and the only part of us equipped to be the executive for the personality—chairperson of the committee of three: the parent, the adult, and the child. Current here-and-now awareness is the unique contribution of the adult. All of the data-gathering homework suggested is adult activity—learning where we have come from and what kind of person we want to be. Self-awareness and self-modification are impossible without a functioning adult. Learning from our own experiences, making good decisions, gathering data from the external world plus awareness of the child and parent parts of ourselves, are the proper functions of our adult.

EXERCISE FOR UNDERSTANDING THE ADULT INSIDE

Make a collage of who you are now—a pictorial representation of yourself. Cut out twenty-five to fifty pictures or words from magazines and newspapers that represent each aspect of you. Organize the pictures, picking the best pictures to represent each area of your life so that the whole collection of pictures is you. Take special time in picking the individual pictures and pore over the arrangement of the whole until you feel it represents you as you are now. Share your collage with a partner and have them ask you questions about the meaning of individual pictures and/or the arrangement.

EXERCISE IN SELF-PERCEPTION

This exercise uses imagination. Some people do not think well in pictures, so if it is difficult for you don't worry. It doesn't mean that there is something wrong with you—not everybody can do this sort of thing well. Complete the exercise the best you can, and follow the instructions. After we have finished we will process it and write it down. Use either a tape recording of the instructions or have a friend lead you through this exercise. Go through this at a leisurely pace.

Close your eyes and begin by taking a few deep breaths. Breathe deeply, exhale completely. Roll your head around a little to relax some of the muscles in your shoulders. Wind down, just relax. For the next few minutes you are not going to have to think about anything. I am going to lead you where you need to go. Follow the instructions and don't worry about making anything happen.

We are going to visit an art gallery. This gallery is very special so you will want to pay particular attention to everything you see. This is your gallery. I want you to see yourself climbing a long flight of stairs in front of a large building. When you get to the top of the stairs there is a small landing and a large set of double doors. As you step forward to open the doors, pause to look at them. They are magnificent works of art. You are aware that the place you are entering is a place of special significance and beauty. . . .

You open the doors and step into a courtyard. The sun is warm and there are plants all around. The most important thing about this courtyard is its peacefulness and tranquility. You are the only person there and the only sounds you hear are the sounds of your own feet. Walk around the courtyard and soak up some of the peacefulness, tranquility, and beauty. . . .

Directly across the courtyard from the large double doors where you came in is a single door that is closed. Walk over to that door and open it. When you open the door it is dark on the other side, but go ahead and step through the door, close it behind you, and stand there with your hand on the doorknob to let your eyes adjust to the darkness. As your eyes begin to adjust you realize that the room is not totally dark, but that it is a very long, narrow room. On each side of this room are paintings. The paintings are individually lighted so that when you walk up to them you can see them very clearly, but the walkway down the center is dimly lit. Take a moment for your eyes to adjust and then begin to walk down your gallery going from side to side looking at the paintings. Just scan each picture, do not stop to study any one painting. . . .

By now you have made it quite a way down this long, narrow room and I want you to look all the way to the far end of the room in the same direction you have been walking. There you will see a bright light. Walk straight toward that light. As you approach it you realize that a spotlight from the ceiling, a floodlight, is throwing a bright light on the floor, and in the middle of that light is a statue of yourself. Study your statue. Walk around it. Notice everything about it—posture, clothing, what it is made of, expression on the face. . . . Be aware of how you feel about your statue—what you like and what you don't like about it as you study it closely. Look at your statue from every angle. Move in close. Stand back. . . .

Walk up and stand beside your statue. Step into the statue. As of this instant you and the statue are one. How do you experience being your statue? You are not just a little person inside a big statue, you are the statue. How do you feel being the statue? Listen to your thoughts and your feelings. . . . Step out of your statue and study it again just like you did the first time. Only this time be aware of any ways in which the statue appears to be different or any ways that you feel differently or think differently about your statue. Look at it from all perspectives. Be aware of your thoughts and feelings. . . .

We are going to leave in just a few moments. If there is anything you want to check out with this statue do it now. . . . Then say good-bye to your statue, turn and start walking out of the long, narrow room. Don't stop to look at any of the other pictures; your business at the gallery is finished. You come to the door at the end of the room, open it, and step out into the courtyard. Pause, and let your eyes adjust to the bright sunlight. Then make your way across the courtyard through the double doors you came in and start walking down that long flight of stairs. When you are ready, open your eyes.

Get a pencil and some paper. In this exercise, the statue is what counts. I want you to write down information on the following questions. You can use shorthand, phrases, words, whatever, but I want you to recover your thoughts and impressions.

1. First, describe your statue in detail, everything you can remember about it when you first saw it. Write down enough information so that if you look back a week from now and try to remember your statue, you can recall it vividly because of the description you are now writing.

2. The next thing is how you felt when you first saw the statue. What was your feeling toward it? You described the statue as you saw it, now write your reaction in terms of your thoughts and feelings. What did you like and not like about the statue?

3. What was it like inside the statue? How did you experience that? What were the thoughts that came to your mind and the feelings you experienced?

4. When you stepped out of the statue how did you feel? How did it feel to be outside of the statue after having been inside of it?

5. Lastly, as you looked at the statue after having been inside it, had it changed any? Had your feelings about it changed after the experience of being in it?

The point of this is simple. You are the statue and the visitor to the gallery. The purpose is to determine (1) how you see yourself—when you had the opportunity to see yourself, to construct yourself, how did you do it?—and (2) how you relate to yourself—how do you feel about the company of your own statue, both being inside it and observing it?

The following is a dialogue I had with workshop participants about what they experienced with their statues. Perhaps this will help you to process and interpret your experience.

Gloria: I would like to talk with you about my statue because I really had some weird feelings with mine. When I first saw the statue I realized it was a picture of myself this morning. I just had on my blue jeans and a shirt, and my hair was long and straight. I was looking forward with my hands down. But I felt, and I don't know if this is what I felt at first or what I realized I felt after, that it was really innocent, happy, and peaceful. I was really comfortable and I really liked it. Then I got inside and I felt really uncomfortable. I just really got the creeps. What I realized when I got inside was that it was a child. There was no adult in there at all. It was a statue of a child. And though it was a picture of me this morning, here I am twenty-nine years old, it was a statue of a child. I felt very wrong, like there was something out of alignment there, and I wanted to get out. Then I got out.

Del: Describe the feeling of uncomfortableness and nervousness that you had.

Gloria: I just felt like there was something wrong, that I was not where I should be. While the picture had looked so good before because I always knew where I was—married and with a family—it was like I ought to be further along. But I felt not at ease with the development, that I was still this innocent child with ideals and a happy childhood.

Del: When you got out of the statue, what was that like for you?

Gloria: Then I didn't feel any comfort or peace. All of a sudden I looked at the statue and there was no age in it. As I said, it was a child. It was more child-size than adult. It had childlike features. I was looking at myself like I had never gone inside. I really enjoyed looking at the statue and I wanted to go back in. I really rebel against that, I guess because I don't feel like I'm still a child. At least I think I don't feel like I'm still a child. When you said how do I see myself, I said I guess I see myself as a child. So I'm baffled.

Del: Why don't you tell me what you learned from this in terms of how you see yourself and how you relate to yourself?

Gloria: Well, as I said I have a hard time because I really loved every minute of my childhood. And while I have feelings of "having to do," I cannot figure out where my parents might have put that upon me because they were telling me more not to do than to do. Then you talk about the nonverbal things so now I'm going to have to run that one through. But I just feel like my whole childhood was really ideal. So what I am doing now is trying to see how I take that ideal of how life ought to be and the American way of how things happen—you go to college, get married, have children, grow old, and live happily ever after—and handle a situation when something goes wrong. It's not so much the big things that I have trouble with, because my mother died when I was seventeen and I have dealt with that. So not everything has been perfect in my life. But I think that I don't handle little situations well. When something goes wrong or not according to my ideal package, I get very bugged by that. And I want things to go well, so I guess in a sense I am a child because I guess that is how children look at things. They expect things to happen in a certain way. And I do, I expect things to go a certain way. And when I fall short, while I don't feel like I hate myself because I don't feel that unhappy with myself, rather like my statue I feel like a child. So I guess it's the childlike view of the world I've got to work on. I don't like that I look at things as a child does.

Del: Yes, I think that there is something about maturity that brings richness and wisdom to life. Yet somehow that isn't imprinting itself upon you. You saw yourself virtually full-sized. You looked like an adult, except in retrospect there were no aging signs, just like all the powerful and precious experiences of life that you have gone through somehow are not registering. It is like you want to live in this idealized world rather than learn from the real world. And I think that is your growth task. I think you have really put your finger on something. I guess if I were to give you a prescription it would be to love that little girl.

Gloria: But see, that's what I think I do too much.

Del: It didn't sound like it. I don't mean to love the situation or your childhood. Rather love the child, love that little girl inside right now. I suspect she suffers a lot of anxiety and scars, and some insecurity about being called upon to face the demands of the adult world. I want the adult to love that little girl and take care of her so she feels comfortable.

Betty: When I saw my statue I was very much drawn to her. She was very lovely and dignified. She looked very peaceful and the feeling I had walking around her was that she could have been real even though made of bronze. She had suffered, she had wisdom, she showed an open spirit. I sense about her something of humanness by the fact that she had suffered very much. In fact, an aura of strength was about her being. She wasn't perfect, but it was real and therefore I felt an empathy. When I went inside I could feel all the sensations that she did, and it was comfortable inside the statue. But as I came out and walked around I felt less sure of myself. I was not so sure that the statue was me, that I really had that connection with her. I would like to have believed that I could carry all that out of the gallery with me.

Del: What keeps you from doing that?

Betty: You are the second person this week who has asked me that.

Del: Who else asked you that?

Betty: My therapist.

Del: That makes it a very good question then. What keeps you from doing that?

Betty: I don't know.

Del: Nobody else put her there. You did. It sounds to me like she is the person you would like to be and I think are fully capable of being. But what keeps you? How did you take that away from yourself? You felt attracted to her at first. Inside at first you identified and felt comfortable with her, the sense I was getting was "this is me and I really feel good about this." But when you stepped outside, how did you take that away from yourself?

Betty: I felt unworthy of it.

Del: Yes.

Betty: So how do I change that?

Del: Part of that will change, I would hope simply with the awareness that "This is me. And I do deserve that." I find that that is a very reassuring and reinforcing notion. That is where the action is, with that poor self-image or negative self-esteem. Your image of yourself is very good cognitively, but you feel unworthy. Now it's important for you to watch the quality of your internal dialogue and things that would hold you back from being the person that you can be.

It is one thing to be shown or told that you are valuable. It is something else to actually see yourself and the image coming unconstructed, unbidden. That can be very reinforcing. It is useful when working with people in therapy. If they see themselves in a good place, what is it that keeps them from being that person? Who says that isn't them? So we take away the restraints that keep them from being the person they can be.

REFLECTION ON YOUR STATUE

1. Are you happy with your statue and the way you related to it?
2. What are the things you like?
3. What are the things you would like to change regarding:
   (a) how you appeared
   (b) how you felt about yourself

Remember, this is your statue; you have created it and you can change it.

A WORD ABOUT THE USE OF GUIDED IMAGERY

Guided imagery is a powerful tool for effecting change in the subconscious mind, and as such is subject to abuse. Many cults (religious, psychological, and political) use this technique to elicit greater conformity to the group's goals. Goals is the key word. Like fire, sex and knowledge, this technique can be used for evil (dehumanizing and destructive ends), or it can be used to enhance and enrich our lives. Two tests will effectively determine whether the use of guided imagery is positive or negative. They are:

1. *The Goal.* What is the rationale for using guided imagery, and what is the desired outcome? Beware of group leaders who are reluctant to state the desired outcome of the process and the rationale for the use of guided imagery. Example of goals where the process serves positive human ends are overcoming phobias, improving athletic performance, increasing self-awareness, and improving interpersonal relationships.

2. *Volunteerism.* In guided imagery you are asked to relinquish conscious control of your mind, so be sure you know what you are doing and why. Group pressure and manipulation by a leader are often used to keep you from thinking for yourself. As long as you are consciously choosing the goal and understand the rationale there is little risk of undue influence. It is always important to make sure that you are not being subjected to group pressure and manipulation in order to get you to cooperate in a guided imagery program.

In doing the guided imagery exercises suggested in this book, feel free to stop whenever you feel uncomfortable. If you experience emotion that you have difficulty controlling or become aware of things that frighten or upset you, stop immediately. Experiences such as these indicate that you could benefit from professional help and should not proceed with further guided imagery without consultation and assistance. Some emotion is to be expected, but if the feelings are extreme and last for several hours, seek professional assistance. This counsel applies to all self-help books. They are not substitutes for the caring guidance of a mental health professional.

PART 4.

Developing the Person Inside

Developing the Person Inside

What do we need to do to change and improve our self-image and self-esteem? We have looked at our past and our present, and must start dealing with some of the weaknesses and distortions that we have identified in our self-image. First, I would like to make a couple of preliminary statements. Adults do learn, change, and grow. Personality is like a plant. Our true selves are always developing and unfolding in response to new experiences at every stage of life. If we are not, we are inhibiting and retarding ourselves. We need to respect the mystery, the depth, and the complexity of human personality. A growing person appreciates the growing richness of personhood.

Some theorists are wrong in their fatalistic attitude toward adult life which is that the die is cast when we are seven or eight, and we are doomed to live out those dynamics. The fact is that we do not have to stay in unsatisfactory patterns of behavior unless we choose to. Some people have a hard time understanding and accepting this. There are several reasons why people choose not to change and stay with an unpleasant or unsatisfactory situation. One reason is that change is scary. A second reason is that we tend to develop an at-home feeling with our problems. It is often safer to cling to a known evil than to exchange it for an unknown good. We don't know exactly what it will be like if we assume responsibility for ourselves. There is a kind of neurotic payoff in being dependent and looking to other people to take care of us and then being mad at them because they didn't do a good job. We can feel self-righteous about that—"If I were doing it I would do a good job." If that's the case then we need to do it, not just talk about it. But there is an element of fear because we have to assume responsibility for our own failures and successes. So there are many reasons why people prefer to stay with a painful and poor self-image rather than work on growth.

Another reason people don't change is because they do not know how to change. This book will be most helpful for these people—those who are not stuck in a debilitating struggle with their own internal conflicts or inadequacies.

The strategies for changing self-image and self-esteem that follow are not the last or only words on the subject. Spiritual experience, Bible study, prayer, and caring groups make enormous contributions to the way we think and feel about ourselves. Most of the people I see in therapy are involved in church and have pastoral guidance. My intent is to put together techniques for change which focus on psychological needs and problems. My contribution, along with other Christian marital health professionals, to spiritual growth lies in discerning spiritual from psychological problems and determining which techniques for growth and change are appropriate. As a pastor I experienced great frustration applying spiritual disciplines to what I now understand to be psychological problems. I interpreted the lack of success as evidence of a lack of belief or insincerity on the parishioner's part, not on my ignorance and lack of skill. Now I see the importance of psychological growth becoming a part of church educational programs. This book was developed from workshops that were designed for and implemented in church settings.

UPDATING THE SELF-IMAGE

How do we change and improve our self-image? The most obvious and simple way of improving self-image is to update it. We need to keep our learned self in synchronization with our true self. That means that we need to take inventory of ourselves every few years. We are not the same persons we were five, ten, or twenty years ago. We change, grow, and need to periodically take inventory of new skills, new interests, new needs, and new perspectives that come to us. We need to incorporate these changes into our personal styles and accept changes as being expected and valid. The anxious person tries to stop the clock. He doesn't want things to change. He wants things to stay the way they were and tries to keep things in a particular frame of reference rather than accept and prosper from growth, development, and change. We need to honor the discoveries that we make.

I hope that you have learned something from this book and profited in discovering a new need, a new interest, a new potential, or a new vision for yourself. I hope you will incorporate this into updating your awareness of who you are as a person and realize that your self-image can change. The adult who sees herself as a little girl in a grown-up body does not have to continue that distortion of her self-image. She can believe the reality that she is an adult who has this frightened, needy child part of her that she has been allowing to run her life. With the adult in charge we can change, develop, and grow. We are not fated or stuck; change is achievable. We have to work for it, but it is possible. It represents a goal to work toward and a task or challenge that is laid out before us. By honoring the discoveries we make along the way we are able to keep our self-image up-to-date.

We all go through a midlife passage. The passage that is poorly handled becomes a crisis. Rather than changing, growing, and keeping ourselves up-to-date with who we are and what it is we really want, we suppress our emerging self until we wake up one day at forty or forty-five or maybe a little earlier or a little later and say "What is it all about? There isn't anything that I am doing that I like." So impulsively we sell the house or hop on a motorcycle and head for the wild blue yonder, just to get away from it. I really advocate an openness to change and a continual evaluation of lifestyle—what is satisfying, what do we want—and if we are not getting enough of what we want, find out why not and how we can go about getting it. We need to monitor ourselves and look at our adult activities. What are we excluding from our lives that we would like to have and what do we need to change?

We need to assume responsibility for developing ourselves. There are two keys we need to look for or look at. One is pain and the other is excitement. We can be pushed by pain—"I hate my job"—or we can be drawn by excitement and new interests into our own future. Both of these are valid motivations. One way of staying alive, of keeping our self-image up-to-date, our lives current, and our lifestyle fitting with our needs, is to place more emphasis on what we want within the framework of our own value structure and value system. This is possible provided that our values are not neurotic, unrealistic, or just introjections from other people's heads into ours. I don't like to see people go against their own values. Values are very important for the structure of character and enable us to channel our energies and define the self. Our values are important, but so are our wants. The child part of us continually needs to be attended to. We need to evaluate what we want and determine how we can get it and stay within our own value system. We must be willing to experiment, to try new things, and listen to new interests.

We also need to listen to our pains. Where do we find the grating dissatisfactions? We need to be aware of our own pain to help us determine and identify what areas we need to be looking at in order to make changes.

UPDATING THE SELF-IMAGE EXERCISE

1. Make a list of things you really enjoy doing or think you would enjoy doing. Make the list in two columns. Column 1 will be "Tried and True" and Column 2 will be "Wish I Could." After each entry in the "tried" column put a date beside it for approximately the last time you engaged in this activity. In the "wish" column put down the reasons why you have not done each of these activities.
2. Make a list of the ways in which you are like your parents or parent-substitutes as you remember them from childhood (not the way they are now, but as you remember them back then). You might want to include influential aunts or uncles, grandparents, or older siblings. Now put a plus by those characteristics which you like in yourself and a minus by those which you do not like or wish you could change. What do you want to do about the minuses? Put your thoughts on paper.
3. Update your current self-image. Is your self-image stuck in some stage of your past or is it current?

Put a descriptive word next to each of the stages below that apply to you.

Preschool
Elementary school
Jr. High School
High School
College

Young Adulthood
30s
40s
50s

Below are some stages people often get stuck in. Do any of these apply to you?

Young athlete (football star, etc.)
Clown
Good little boy/girl
Teenage sex symbol
One most likely to succeed
Class goof-off
School failure

Which of these descriptive words do you feel is closest to your self-image? Is it outdated?

In updating our self-image we need to make sure that our awareness of our picture of "who we are" doesn't reflect a past stage in our lives, but a present stage in our lives. To keep our self-image up-to-date, we need to continually examine and check out new interests to see who we really are, what comes up in us, what it is that we need now that we didn't need five years ago, and how we are going to go about meeting that need.

INTERNAL DIALOGUE

After updating our self-image we need to improve the quality of our internal dialogue. The way we talk to ourselves and relate to ourselves is crucial to the way we see ourselves, (our self-image) and the way we feel about ourselves, (our self-esteem). It is important to acknowledge that there is within each of us an internalized parent, an internalized adult, and an internalized child. There is potentially a critical parent or a nurturing parent, and a natural child or an adaptive child within each of us. The parent is always sending messages such as, "you should," "you ought to," "why are you?" "don't you think that?" "you must," "you have to." That's the language of the parent. It is always giving orders and stating rules, many of which are valuable, but many may not be valuable.

If we have a poor self-image, do not see ourselves in a positive light, and do not feel good about ourselves, it is probably the result of the quality of our internal dialogue. The critical parent keeps telling our child, "You are no good, you are a loser," or "Why did you do that?"and "Are you ever going to succeed?" It keeps questioning and raising doubts. Many times a part of the critical parent is the doubter, who is never going to let you relax and think you can move ahead with any confidence. To change the quality of the internal dialogue the adult must intervene and intercept those messages, and make the parent talk to the adult. Every time there is a "you should" "you ought" "you have to" "you must" "why are you doing that?" message, the adult needs to say,"Who says I have to?" "Who says I ought to?" "Who wants to know?" If you decide that the adult says that you ought not to, that message gets passed to the child. "No you may not do that. I have decided that this prohibition is a valid part of my value structure." On the other hand, there may be a lot of "you ought to do this" and you can say, "That's nonsense. That sounds like something my father would have told me" or "That's just my mother needling me along. And I don't agree with that. She was wrong then, or maybe she was right then, but she's wrong now. I am going to discount that message."

One of the distortions that arise out of this is that we talk to ourselves in a negative and demeaning way. The means of control used to keep us from doing certain things has been by putting ourselves down, intimidating, and overemphasizing guilt and fear. As adults we must decide why we behave in particular ways and subscribe to certain norms and values that are informed by the here and now rather than just acting out of childhood fears. The adult is responsible to evaluate the negative information that comes from the parent. I want to emphasize again that the parent is an essential part of us. A person who does not have a functioning internalized parent has serious personality problems. But if the internal parent functions in a demeaning and critical way it can be the source of great pain as well as guidance, protection, and control. The adult part of us, our unique self based on our own experiences, needs to evaluate this legacy from the past and decide which of the values our parents subscribed to and culture subscribes to that we will also subscribe to.

It may well be that 75 to 80 percent of what we have learned is valid and as an adult we can agree to such things as, "I am an American, I believe in saluting the flag, I have great respect for our American traditions, free enterprise, democratic principles, and protection of the rights of minorities." We can decide that these things which are not valued in other cultures are important to us. Much of the past, many of the things I believed when I was six or seven years of age, I still believe and probably will believe until the day I die. But the majority of things that I believed at age six have changed, simply because as an adult I have analyzed them and they do not fit with my adult experience.

It is important for us to review all of our internal dialogue and to continually review it so that we keep the information accurate and up-to-date. In this way we do not allow the negative means, the critical parent, to cause us to feel badly, especially when the point of those messages has been lost. For example, my mother called me stupid because she wanted me to work harder at learning math. Even though I learned to do math well, the message of having been called stupid remains. I feel badly about myself because I believe I am stupid. The name is there, the image is there, but it is being used out of context. So we need to evaluate those messages because much pain comes from those tapes that are no longer within context. The lies and distortions are passed on to us because of our parents' fears, ignorance, and the misinformation they taught us. When that becomes a part of us through our own internalized parent, it is so authoritative that it seems like it is the voice of God. Often these authoritative voices concern trivial things, such as whether you ride your bike clockwise or counterclockwise in your own backyard. However, it does make a difference whether you drive your car on the right- or left-hand side of the street, depending on whether you are in the United States or Great Britain. The results could be tragic if you don't have the rules straight. The adult part of us is responsible for making the distinction, but the rules need to be accurate and up-to-date.

There is a difference between hearing the internal parent that we think is the voice of God and being able to discern the true voice of God through responsible Bible study. In the Christian life, part of our adult function is to inform our parent based upon responsible Bible study. When we find childish or inappropriate notions or teachings from our past they need to be revised, corrected, and related to new data. This updating leads to Christian maturity. God is not glorified by our insisting that our all-too-human internal voices are His.

We need to remember that what we are dealing with here is a tape recorder and we can turn the messages off. We can not do it quickly or simply. It takes time, but we can do it. We can reprogram the tapes with good messages, so we don't have to work as hard to monitor our internal dialogue. It is almost like a dialysis machine. You have to pull the blood out in order to purify it before it can be sent back into the system. Once the kidneys begin to catch hold and the blood is O.K., you can allow the blood to go back to the ordinary circulatory system. Much the same principle works within us. We need to consciously think about whether or not the messages we are feeding ourselves are healthy or toxic.

Some of the things to look for in our internal dialogue are critical and demeaning statements. Do we call ourselves names such as stupid, no good, or do we tell ourselves we can't do anything right? We need to look for statements which are critical or demeaning to ourselves. Those statements need to be evaluated and eliminated. They do not do any good. There is no point in cursing ourselves, abusing ourselves, or brow-beating ourselves. We all have a tendency to do it and we all need to work at eliminating it.

Another thing we need to watch for is our expectations. Many times the parent has expectations for what the child ought to be and what we ought to be. Some of these are unrealistic. The point is that the critical parent inside will never be satisfied. Many times our own live parents have had high expectations for us that we just could not meet, so we felt like failures. Yet we continue in adult life to treat ourselves the same way our parents treated us, with high expectations and demands that we could never meet. So we always tell ourselves "You could have done better," "You should have done more." We end up whipping ourselves when we need to be saying to ourselves, "I don't deserve this whipping. Who says I have to be a particular way? Here I am at forty years of age and who is defining who I am?" It is better to assume that responsibility ourselves and reevaluate the expectations, perhaps lowering them or changing them the way we want to. Unrealistic expectations are divorced from reality and keep us feeling negatively about ourselves. I think Lloyd Ogilvie is right when he says, "Discouragement is the illegitimate child of false expectations." There are also expectations such as being told, "You are never going to make it. You basically are no good. You can't do anything right. Nothing ever seems to work out for you." We end up feeling like victims who can't do anything right. Negative and unrealistic expectations are toxic to our internal dialogue and need to be carefully weeded out from our thoughts.

Another thing we need to listen to in our internal dialogue is whining, including wishing—the "if onlys"—where we end up blaming others or playing poor me. This is nothing more than a child looking for a rescuer. Our child ends up whining and the adults needs to assume responsibility by saying,"Talk to me about what it is you expect. If the expectations are negative or unrealistic, we will change them, but I am not going to go through life whining and looking to blame someone else for the lot that I am in." So the task is to put the adult in charge, make the parent talk to the adult and the adult talk to the child.

INTERNAL DIALOGUE EXERCISE

1. List the names you call yourself or the putdowns you use on yourself when you are frustrated, disappointed, or angry.
2. Note the shoulds, oughts, musts, and have-tos you say to yourself. How do they compare in frequency with the I wants or I am choosings?

3. List the words you use to encourage, teach, and guide yourself. Do you seek to lead or drive yourself through life?

Now take your list from No. 1 and for every putdown and name you have listed ask, "What is the evidence for this? Am I dumb just because my parent says I am? Do I always fail to finish things?" Confront those that are untrue as being wrong, and balance those that are partially true with some of the words and thoughts you have from list No. 3. This will help produce a more balanced and accurate diet of self-analysis and appraisal.

Concerning list No. 2, our shoulds and oughts are very important, but they are often overworked and misapplied. The purpose of this inventory is to make sure that we are guiding, not inhibiting ourselves with the shoulds and oughts. By questioning the shoulds and oughts the adult keeps the parent purged of out-of-date, distorted, or false information. There are things we ought to do and we deserve to feel guilty if we do not do them. However, things like eating breakfast, taking a day off from work, or expressing feelings of anger and disappointment are simply matters of choice and do not have great moral significance. The shoulds and the oughts should be reserved for those issues which we affirm in our here-and-now adult as being our moral values.

REPARENTING

The healing power of the imagination is an essential tool for self-understanding and change. It is a part of our mental capacity that often gets us into trouble (imagined fears, projections, distorted memories, etc.), but seldom is enough attention paid to the imagination as a tool for healing and change. Logical, rational thought and understanding are important, but they are not our only ways of thinking, conceptualizing, and understanding.

Children rely almost exclusively on the imagination—wishing, hoping, and daydreaming. They think in pictures, rather than with symbols. Much of what we think and feel about ourselves is rooted in the child part of us, still held captive in this basic primary process of thinking—imagination. If we are going to change the way we feel about ourselves, we must change the pictures we have of ourselves as well as the beliefs about ourselves. When beliefs about ourselves and feelings about ourselves are not congruous, it usually means that we have pictures of ourselves that are hidden from conscious view. To correct these we must use imagination. We must speak and think in the language of small children, the language in which children store the most powerful messages.

Reparenting the self requires an extensive examination of the childhood and adolescent years to locate the misinformation and distortions that we have internalized. We must learn to care for the child, meet his needs, and earn his trust. To do this we must provide him with some corrective and helpful emotional experiences—these must be done on his turf, in his language of pictures and feelings, not in the cognitive language of the adult.

The adult part of us uses rational and verbal skills to deal with our internalized parent. The adult part also uses imagination, simple concepts, and nonverbal tools in dealing with the child part of us. What we have is an educational process designed to fill in the gaps or correct the distortions in our own developmental process. Since the adult part of us is in touch with reality and can learn from here and now experiences, it is the part we relate to and teach how to retrain the parent and child parts of our personalities.

The challenge is to use the basic principles of Christian

love and growth to guide the way in which we relate to the parent and child parts of ourselves. We must learn to love and accept ourselves not with an "if" kind of love, or a "because" kind of love, but with an "in spite of" kind of love. This is the way God loves us; not because of what we have done or unusual attributes within ourselves. He loves us in spite of what we have done. We are valuable persons no matter what has befallen us in life. We need to be able to speak the truth in love to ourselves as well as to others. The critical parent may speak in truth, but has not learned God's loving touch of speaking the truth in love.

REPARENTING EXERCISE 1

1. What are the most painful emotions you experience?
2. What is it about yourself that you like the least and like the best?
3. How and to whom do you express your emotions, especially affection, anger, and fear?

For each of the following questions, picture instances in your life that illustrate or verify each statement.

1. Picture yourself in emotional pain. What happened and how did you deal with it?
2. Recall times when (a) the aspect of yourself that you like best was in charge, and (b) the aspect of yourself that you like least was in charge.
3. Think about times in your life when you expressed your feelings and jot down what happened. How did others respond to your self-disclosure and how did you feel about their responses? What decisions did you make concerning feelings and their expression as a result of these experiences?

Please do this work carefully before you proceed to the next exercise.

REPARENTING EXERCISE 2

I would like you to get in touch with the child part of yourself. This is another exercise in self-perception involving the imagination. First of all get comfortable, but have a pen and paper handy because after you complete this I want you to write down your experience. Use a tape recording with instructions or have a friend lead you through this exercise. It is best to go through this at a leisurely pace.

Close your eyes and concentrate on your breathing. Feel the air rushing through your nostrils, filling your lungs, expanding your chest, and then the sense of relaxation as the air whooshes out through your throat and your nose. Create a sense of isolation with your eyes shut.

Next picture yourself as a child doing something typical for you, playing in the barn, your bedroom, the backyard, going for a hike or over to a friend's house, maybe to your treehouse, wherever you as a child typically spent time. You might want to imagine two or three pictures just to find the one that seems to fit your child on a typical day. . . .

Settle on one picture. Then, as an adult enter the picture but remain invisible to your child. I want you to go and just watch the child part of you as he/she was playing on that day a long time ago. The child is by himself/herself, and you are just observing, watching. What are your impressions of this child? How do you feel as you watch him/her at play or work? Take as much time as you need to visualize these things. . . . Now, become visible to your child. The child looks up and sees you. You are dressed exactly as you are today, stepping back into the world of your own childhood. Go over to the child, set the child at ease, and begin to talk with him/her. Instinctively the child part of you trusts you, and begins to talk with you, responding to your questions. Explore problems with the child part of you. Encourage him/her to talk with you about how he/she feels about things, what is troubling, what is disconcerting, what is upsetting to him/her. Do not be surprised by the strong emotional content to some of this experience. The child is not always what it seems to be and it is seldom without pain. . . .

I want you to be a wise and caring friend to this little boy or little girl. I want you to give him/her feedback, try to help, and encourage him/her to discuss with you a variety of problems. Don't be afraid to probe—you know this child very well. Just take some time with your child; be willing to dig a little bit. . . .

We are not going to spend much more time with your child of the past. If there is anything else that needs to be said, another question asked or a comment made, a subject discussed, do it. Again, take as much time as it is necessary for this step. . . .

It is time to say good-bye to the little boy or little girl with whom you have been talking. I want you to be reinforcing. Underscore any important messages you have left with the child or that you would like to leave with the child. Assure the child that you will be back, that you will spend more time talking with him/her and being with him/her. But most importantly, assure that little boy or little girl that whenever he or she needs you, you will be there, and that you will step back into his/her life when he/she needs you.

Hug the child, turn, and start walking away. Open your eyes. Take your paper and your pen, and without talking to anyone write down your response to the following questions:

1. How do you feel about what you have just experienced and what you have just done? Right now, as an adult, what is the predominant feeling tone inside you?

2. Next, write down the problems you explored. What did you talk about? What issues did you and your child of the past discuss?
3. Write down what your child was like. What was your general impression of this little boy or little girl?
4. After talking with him/her, what did you think your child needed more of than he/she was getting, or less of then he/she was getting?
5. Describe the relationship that you feel you had for those few moments with your inner child of the past.

As another exercise, I would like for you to do the same experience again, remembering yourself as an adolescent, a teenager. Go back and visit yourself at that point in your life. What were the concerns that you were experiencing then? Again do it in pictures. There is something powerfully and emotionally vivid about remembering in pictures rather than just writing down memories. Visualize yourself the best you can at that period of time.

There are two main reasons why this is an important exercise. One is that you begin to become acquainted with your internalized child, for the child you imagine is the child who is still in residence within you. Secondly, it is a tool for understanding how you are doing emotionally at any point in time. This may seem strange, but it is true. The child inside of us is our emotional thermometer for how we are feeling. The ability to imagine is natural for us; therefore, we can use it for our growth. For example, in an argument with a loved one we may become aware that we are feeling tense and angry. If we are able to be by ourselves and picture the child from our past, the child within us, perhaps we will see an angry, helpless child who has been unjustly punished by a stepparent. The argument with the loved one has triggered an old tape, and we feel like a helpless child. When we can picture what is going on we can use our here-and-now adult to help solve the problem. First, through our imagination, we can enter that child's world and stand up for our child against the stepparent or other abusing person. We can offer our child that love, protection, and security it did not experience as a child. Using the pictures of the child's world, using our imagination, we can start changing the emotional reality of our inner child.

The second thing our adult can do is recognize that we are not helpless, and we can choose not to behave that way. Thus, the imagining, the reparenting forms a base for changing our emotions by changing our own child's tapes. We are aware of what the old emotional child's tapes are so we can begin choosing to act differently.

The concept of reparenting, which means to retrain our internalized child, is difficult to communicate through the printed word, but when grasped and used is one of the most powerful tools available in changing self-image.

REPARENTING EXERCISE 3

We begin the process of reparenting by visiting the child within or visiting the teenager within, and talking and spending time getting to know him. What I would like you to do now is to think of a time in your childhood or early adolescence when you were really hurting. A time when things weren't going right, you were upset, friends had rejected you, something bad was going on, something that as you think about it now brings you negative feelings. It is something that is fresh, it is so much a part of you. Spend a few moments combing through your memory and come up with an event or incident in childhood or early adolescence when you were hurting. Use a tape recording with instructions or have a friend lead you through this exercise. Go through this at a leisurely pace.

Begin by taking a few moments to relax and clear your mind. Focus on your breathing, fill your lungs full and exhale slowly several times. Relax your muscles by tightening them and letting go. Seek out every tense muscle and relax it. Think of your mind as an electric motor, and turn the switch off and feel it slow down. Relinquish control of your neck, hands, legs, and face. Just let them go. We are going to revisit that place and experience the pain of that moment, that hour, just as you did then. In your mind you are this child, this little boy or little girl. While you are going through this experience, feel those feelings. Think for a moment about what you would like to have had done in this situation. If someone is beating on you, perhaps you would like someone to defend you. If someone has hurt you, maybe you would like someone to comfort you. If someone has abandoned you and rejected you, maybe you would like someone to be your friend. If someone has misunderstood you, perhaps you would like someone to really care about you, care for you, and try to understand. . . .

At this instant, the big you, dressed just like you are now, comes into that situation. You remain the little boy or the little girl, and the big you comes in and does the very thing that you wished had been done years ago. If someone needs to be confronted and told off about the way they are treating you, the big part of you does that. If the little you needs to be comforted, the big part of you does that. He or she knows exactly what to do.

After the big you has accomplished his or her task—the confrontation or the encounter has been completed, and the comforting has been done, the big part of you takes the very little you in his or her arms and holds him or her. Then the big you says something very important to the little boy or the little girl, and that is "Any time you need me, I will be here. Remember that." And with that he or she slowly leaves.

With your eyes still closed, reflect upon this experience, mainly upon how you feel.

1. How did you feel the first time you relived this experience?
2. How do you feel now having gone through it the second time and having the protection, support, and wisdom of the big you?

The process of growing up and the process of changing our self-image and reparenting ourselves begins at the point where we say to ourselves, "I do not have to continue to treat myself in the way in which I was treated." We parent ourselves in the way we were parented. If we were well-parented we say good things to ourselves, we take good care of ourselves, we parent ourselves well and we don't have to think about it. But when we are not parenting ourselves well and we are experiencing emotional pain, then it is important that the adult part of us learns how to be a good parent. The adult has to interrupt the messages, break up the cycle, reprogram and retape the message in the parent.

The essence of change is educating the adult and realizing that we do have a choice. We do not have to continue putting ourselves down, belittling ourselves, expecting too much of ourselves, demanding all sorts of things from ourselves without fighting back, without making a change. It is important to look back and see what was going on with us during our childhood and adolescent years, because this is where all these messages and feelings come from.

In order to help you understand your experience I have included some discussion verbatim from a workshop about what people had to share from their experiences in doing this exercise.

Del: What was this exercise like for you? How did you experience it?

Mary: I felt safe.

Del: You felt safe. What did you feel before?

Mary: Frightened, angry.

Del: If you were to think along the course of your life would you say there have been a good many times when you felt frightened and angry? And many times, as you look back upon it, if you felt like you had been able to take care of yourself that you wouldn't have felt that way?

Mary: It was quite a difference.

Del: Let me also point out that nothing happened outside of you. It was all something you did inside, you comforted and protected yourself until you felt safe. No one else did it for you. A lot of times when we feel unsafe, insecure or unsure of ourselves those feelings come from within us, they are tapes from years ago, and if we are going to change the way we feel about ourselves the way to do it is to go back and relive some of those experiences.

Eric Berne says that the doing of therapy is redoing the past in the present in order to free us for the future. If we do not change those feeling tapes we end up repeating them and reliving them and having to deal with them over and over again. So this is basically a cleaning up process. We so often relive a tape which is no longer appropriate, because the fact of the matter is that if you feel frightened during this exercise, it means that you are still feeling somewhat toward yourself as you felt when you were a child or an adolescent. But the fact is that you are an adult now and you can protect yourself and filter out reasonable from unreasonable fear. You do not have to live with the feeling that you are a helpless child who doesn't have anyone to protect you.

Cindy: I thoroughly enjoyed the fantasy. It was so good to find a big friend who took an interest in me.

Del: How did you feel before you met that friend?

Cindy: I had feelings of fear and insecurity.

Del: You as an older and wiser friend were a source of encouragement, comfort, and strength to yourself. We can always be our own friend and we need to be our own best friend. It really changes the quality of our internal life when we do, and it is a way of enhancing self-esteem, changing some of those negative feeling tapes.

Rhoda: I had a hard time coming up with my situation, but then when I thought about it the situation was that I didn't make cheerleader and I was really disappointed. I felt very self-conscious and like I was ugly and bow-legged. My mother and my brothers told me the same things that I as my older person in the fantasy told myself. And I believed myself where I hadn't believed them, because mothers always tell you that it's better that you didn't make cheerleader . . . but I believed myself.

Del: That is an interesting phenomenon because it bears out the idea that it isn't just what happened to you, it is how you interpret it that counts. Here your mother tried to comfort you but you discounted it with "mothers always say that" and "she has to, it's her job to do that." But when you did it for yourself you knew what your motivation was and you believed yourself. And that's why many of the things that need to be changed deep inside us don't happen when other people tell us. That is why advice doesn't work so well unless we take it and apply it to ourselves, incorporate it into our internal dialogue.

Larry: The older me took the place of my parents. The older me did something that I wanted them to do but that they didn't do.

Del: It's a way of filling the gaps or compensating for those things that were lacking in the parenting that we experienced as children. That's why it is very important for us to understand what went on within us in those periods of childhood and adolescence. As adults we can be to ourselves what it is that we need to be, and not just repeat the patterns of parenting ourselves that came from the example of our parents. We can compensate for a deficit or a failure.

Kathy: There was something happening to me in the presence of my parents and after my big person came to talk to my little person and left I thought, "Boy, now I'm really going to get it from Mom and Dad because I brought this other person in to undergird me and comfort me, and they aren't going to like that."

Del: So you came out of it with kind of a negative feeling, didn't you? O.K., what I would suggest you do is go back and do this again, only this time have the big you turn and tell your parents what she thinks of the way that they have been treating you. They could have intervened; they could have done what the big you did, but they didn't do it. I think that the little girl inside of you needs to know that the big you will protect her, and not only comfort her and get her through her own internal trauma, but will actually stand up to set things right. She can stand up for her and I think you will feel better inside feeling that you can protect yourself.

Some may think that these exercises are childish and trivial. It is hard to communicate in written form the enormous power and healing potential they have. I have been amazed over the past several years of the power that imagining and reparenting can have in the therapeutic and healing process. Here we have only lightly touched on the technique for your own personal growth, whereas in a therapeutic situation there is more interaction between client and therapist, and the exercise can be tailored and controlled to meet an individual's needs.

ASSERTIVENESS

Another way of changing self-image and self-esteem involves assertiveness. There are environments that are toxic and poisonous to us. If we are going to grow there are times when we have to assume responsibility for changing the environment that we are in. We first need to assume responsibility for retraining people. People treat us the way we train them to treat us. If we train people to treat us like a doormat or like the family dog, they will continue if we encourage them to treat us that way. If we are going to feel good about ourselves, it is important that we do not tolerate abusive treatment.

Physical and psychological abuse demeans and tears down the self-image. A battered wife will come in and talk with me about the pain she is experiencing and all that she is going through and has endured for years. Inside my mind is the question, "Why in the world would anybody in their right mind tolerate living in an environment like this?" Once you begin to listen, you see how a person's self-image is almost totally decimated and discounted by abusive behavior. Sometimes people actually believe that is what they deserve, that is what is right for them. Their self-image is so weak that they cannot pull themselves up and assert themselves. You need a good self-image to assert yourself, but by the same token to maintain your self-image you need to be able to assert yourself. There are always people who are going to want to take away your freedom, your power, and the influence and happiness that you have gained. Being able to assume responsibility to speak up for yourself, maintain your own borders, seek your own truth, and not blame other people is your responsibility.

Assertiveness is based on three issues:

1. Believing that we are worth being heard.
2. Developing communication skills.
3. Having the courage to put ourselves to the test.

The first issue is what this book is about. The second issue involves the difference between being assertive (acting for me) and aggressive (acting against another to hurt or punish). "I" messages are appropriate for assertiveness because they are personal and sharing. "It" messages are impersonal and vague, whereas "you" messages are blaming. These are often used in aggressive behavior.

The third issue means that we do not give in to the fears that come from the child part of us. We learn by doing. The secret is to start, but start small. Plan to speak up on issues that are not terribly important, make requests that are easily granted, or refuse invitations where not too much is at stake. Be guided by your own level of discomfort as to how fast you move toward more significant action. Remember, the personality is like a muscle. It may hurt when used, but it gets stronger with use.

Internal dialogue and reparenting can also be powerful tools in dealing with irrational fears of others, life and of the consequences of asserting ourselves. Remember, the goal of assertiveness is not to see ourselves as superior to others, simply equal, and to act on that assumption. Many difficulties we have relating to life and to other people stem from irrational and false beliefs we have about ourselves and others. To correct these, we need to identify the statements that we make to ourselves and evaluate them to see if they are true and rational. Some examples of irrational beliefs that often hold people back are:

1. *The opinions of others are important; but my opinions are insignificant.* Even if the opinions of others are more informed and accurate, it does not mean that my opinions are unimportant. Being heard is important to me even if my opinions are less than perfect.

2. *I am not as good as other people; therefore, my opinions, needs, and wants must be deferred to them.* The truth is that we all are lovable and valuable to God and should treat ourselves as such.

3. *Other people, particularly people in authority, know better what is best for me.* At times this is true, but we must assume responsibility for our own happiness and not depend on others to think for us. We need to listen to our own thoughts and feelings as to those of others, and assume responsibility for the choices we make.

4. *If others disagree, that means that I am wrong.* The need to have the agreement of others reflects a lack of confidence in our own judgment. Most opinions are a

mixture of truth and error and sometimes my opinions will be more true than false, and other times more erroneous than valid. My right to speak does not depend on the concurrence of others.

5. *I need the approval of others in order to survive.* This myth causes both unhappiness and frustration. There is no rational relationship between the agreement and approval of others and our value as persons, but if we think we need the approval of others to survive, we make ourselves victims of their whims, opinions, and wants.

The process involves three steps:

1. Identifying the inhibiting message
2. Evaluating and correcting it
3. Consistently substituting the corrected message for the erroneous/outdated message we have been telling ourselves.

The key word is consistency. No matter how good a plan we have, unless we execute it with determination, nothing changes. We must choose to believe the updated and revised message and act on it.

Guided imagery can help us see ourselves as we want to be. If we can see ourselves speaking up for ourselves, confronting aggressive and manipulative people, and correcting unfair situations successfully, we can dispel some of the irrational or childhood fears associated with these activities. We are thus providing ourselves with emotional experiences that encourage rather than discourage assertive behavior.

The process is simple. Think about the situation or person you wish to confront and clearly formulate what you want to achieve by this confrontation. Then construct your speech carefully and concisely. Close your eyes and imagine yourself effectively carrying out this confrontation. You are secure and confident in your approach, clear in stating your thoughts, feelings, and wants to the other person. See yourself dealing with objections effectively and finally getting what you want. How does it feel to be successful? Let the feeling soak in. Just as we need to correct negative beliefs that keep us from asserting ourselves, we also need to correct the negative feelings of fear, dread,and apprehension that hold us back.

I strongly recommend the workshop or group format for doing assertiveness training because both offer opportunities to try out the new behavior and get feedback assessing its effectiveness. Weaknesses can then be specifically identified and worked on. No matter how well we may be prepared intellectually and emotionally, only practice will improve performance.

Positive self-image and self-esteem are basic to assertive behavior, but some people need specific help with assertiveness even after substantial self-image and self-esteem improvement. Seek out a class, workshop or counselor who can help you with your particular difficulty.

ASSERTIVENESS SURVEY

1. Do you feel intimidated by people in authority? Give examples.
2. Do you tend to let people know where you stand, or do you tend to put things aside and hope things will get better?
3. Do you tend to give more than you get in relationships?
4. Which of your needs do you have difficulty communicating to others?
5. Where do you experience more difficulty in speaking up for your rights and needs—at work, at home, with friends, or with strangers? Give examples.

CONCLUSION

We have come to the end of this program for self-discovery and self-development. My hope is that you have clarified some of your self-image needs and have made progress in changing the negative ways in which you think and feel about yourself. It is possible that more issues were raised than were settled. I encourage you to seek the help of a skilled counselor to give you more individual attention in the problem areas.

My hope and prayer for each of you who takes the work of self-discovery and self-development seriously is that you will grow in Christian maturity and usefulness in God's kingdom. God honors responsible efforts toward self-improvement and learning to relate to ourselves as He relates to us in Jesus Christ. Until we experience our own inner healing we are poor tools for helping others.

All of the suggestions for personal growth made in this book will not be helpful to everybody. If some of them help a few of you, I will be deeply gratified.

POSTSCRIPT FOR THE CHURCHES

Most Christians agree that the gospel is authoritative in relating to God, others, and self. If asked to rate the importance of these three areas of relationships, a majority of Christians would put God first, relationship to others second, and the relationship to ourselves as being relatively unimportant. From a clinical point of view, however, the hierarchy is inverted. In other words, our relationship to God (not just our intellectual beliefs about God) and others depends to a large degree on how we relate to ourselves. People who do not love themselves have great difficulty comprehending the love of God much less accepting it and rejoicing in it. Many clients I see are well-intentioned, well-disciplined Christians, who put up a good front but are miserable within themselves. They do not believe they deserve to be loved so they strive to earn God's and other people's acceptance through serving the church. In areas of evangelism, our relationship to God is primary and in considering Christian ethics our relationship to others is primary, but when it comes to growing toward personal maturity as a Christian, our relationship to ourselves is basic.

The educational ministry of the church is sorely deficient because it fails to take self-image—one's relationship to one's self—seriously. Accepting the gospel in depth means that we alter our patterns of thinking and feeling toward ourselves to conform to the thinking and the feelings that God holds toward us. Developing seminars, workshops, and classes on understanding self-image development and offering guidance to change the negative patterns of thinking and feeling is a need that church leadership must respond to.

It seems too much time is spent telling people how they should be and not nearly enough time is spent encouraging people to explore themselves and accept who they are. Until we are able to accept and love ourselves as we are (that is, as God does), we will not experience the abundant life and maturity God intends. Christian growth and development involves both grace and works, but grace

(God's loving acceptance of us and our loving acceptance of ourselves) must be the foundation. Too many of us try to build Christian lives without doing the basic work of learning to love and value ourselves as God does. We strive to become what we think we should be rather than discovering and developing who we are as part of God's good creation.